Classroom Companion: Business

More information about this series at http://www.springer.com/series/16374

Deniz Ozenbas • Michael S. Pagano
Robert A. Schwartz • Bruce W. Weber

Liquidity, Markets and Trading in Action

An Interdisciplinary Perspective

Springer

Deniz Ozenbas
Feliciano School of Business
Montclair State University
Montclair, NJ, USA

Michael S. Pagano
Villanova School of Business
Villanova University
Villanova, PA, USA

Robert A. Schwartz
Zicklin School of Business
Baruch College/CUNY
New York, NY, USA

Bruce W. Weber
Alfred Lerner College of Business and Economics
University of Delaware
Newark, DE, USA

Supplemental material: Powerpoint slides and discussion questions for each chapter are available on the TraderEx website, "http://etraderex.com/"etraderex.com

This book is an open access publication.

ISSN 2662-2866 ISSN 2662-2874 (electronic)
ISBN 978-3-030-74816-6 ISBN 978-3-030-74817-3 (eBook)
https://doi.org/10.1007/978-3-030-74817-3

This Springer imprint is published by the registered company Springer Nature Switzerland AG
The registered company address is: Gewerbestrasse 11, 6330 Cham, Switzerland

Preface

This book addresses four standard business school subjects: microeconomics, finance, macroeconomics, and information systems as they relate to trading, liquidity, transaction costs, and market structure. It also presents an interactive simulation model of equity market trading. What does our treatment of these different subjects have in common? In each, we consider the impact of trading costs and other impediments (that we call "frictions") on market outcomes. A second commonality of the four topics is that each is presented with reference to one specific financial market – the equity market. We also consider the effect of regulation on equity market structure. Addressing these topics can shine a bright light on how a real-world market functions, and your interaction with the simulation tool should be both informative and fun.

Each of the chapters is designed so it can be used as a standalone module in an existing finance, economics, or information science course. But, while each chapter is self-contained, there are common threads across the book. We address an array of key thoughts from different angles, and reading the entire book will enable you to achieve a more comprehensive understanding of the workings of a real-world financial market.

Microeconomics, Chap. 1

In the microeconomics chapter, we invoke a commonly used (but not always explicitly stated) assumption in economics and finance presentations: that buying and selling in a marketplace is *frictionless*. We compare the Capital Asset Pricing Model, a keystone of what has been referred to as "modern portfolio theory," with the standard microeconomics consumer choice model, both of which are based on the assumption that a marketplace is a frictionless environment. We first show, for both models, how the optimal decisions of individual participants (investors in finance and consumers in microeconomics) are made and how equilibrium prices are determined. Then, for the equity market analysis, we introduce one real-world, friction-related constraint on order submission: each participant is allowed to transmit just one order (one price and size) to the market. With this constraint, we show that prices set in the financial marketplace can differ from the equilibrium values theoretically identified in a frictionless model where participants submit complete, continuous curves (downward sloping for buys and upward sloping for sells) to the market. In so doing, we demonstrate one way in which a real-world market and a theoretical market can yield different results.

Finance, Chap. 2

In the finance chapter, we focus on trading, which is the implementation of an investment decision. This is different from stock selection or, more broadly stated, portfolio formation. Portfolio managers decide which stocks (and how much) to buy and to sell. After a portfolio decision has been made, it must be implemented, and especially for handling large orders and navigating stressful markets, specific skills and responsibilities are needed that require the expertise of a professional trader. However, the efficiency with which orders are handled and turned into trades depends, not just on traders' abilities, but also on a market's liquidity, on the design of the marketplace where shares are traded, and on the regulatory environment. Following Chap. 1 where we show how a single market friction can affect participants' behavior and, in so doing, alter market outcomes, in Chap. 2, we expand our focus on marketplace frictions. Underlying the issues dealt with in Chap. 2 is the difficulty investors have evaluating shares when information sets are huge and imperfect. Given this difficulty, different investors form different expectations of stock value and, consequently, share prices have to be discovered in a marketplace. We deal in Chap. 2 with price discovery, with the accentuation of short period volatility that attends price discovery, and with trading costs that are incurred because the marketplace is not frictionless. Chapter 2 also focuses on market design and regulation.

Macroeconomics, Chap. 3

In the macroeconomics chapter, we focus on the dynamics of price discovery following unanticipated macroeconomic information shocks. In so doing, we describe some examples of macroeconomic-related shocks, consider their effects on the U.S. stock market, and zero in on the inter-relationship between financial markets and the macroeconomy. In this chapter, we develop a deeper understanding of how unexpected macroeconomic news can help an investor identify via fundamental analysis which industries (and what firms within those sectors) might perform well in the future. In addition, it is believed by many that the specific timing and placement of trades can be enhanced by employing other techniques such as technical analysis. By applying the concepts and analytical tools described in this chapter, financial assets can be assessed more accurately within real-world financial markets, thus benefiting both investors and society.

Information Systems, Chap. 4

In the information systems chapter, we approach the financial market from a technology perspective. Today's trading desks are heavily dependent on information systems, and a growing subfield of "fintech" is focused on the development and continuing enhancement of computerized trading system infrastructures. Collaboration among the fields of finance, data science, and information systems is substantial, and, in today's high-tech marketplaces and trading rooms, finance and information science professionals regularly work side by side. In this highly innovative and competitive environment, it is crucial that information technology professionals understand the challenge of handling trading desires, and the complexities involved in turning orders into trades at appropriate prices.

Simulated Trading, Chap. 5

This chapter will use the TraderEx trading simulation to demonstrate and "bring to life" the concepts described thus far in this book about trading, liquidity, and market structure. We provide some essential tools that will help you to understand better the challenges you can face when operating in a complex, dynamic environment. A particularly good way to do this is by experiential learning. To this end, we present our trading simulation. With it, you can enter your orders into the simulation's computer-driven market, and see how the decisions you make can affect market prices and the trading outcomes you realize. Each of the four of us has taught courses and run seminars using our simulation software, and the feedback we have received has been strong. A finance student told us that he was surprised by the sizable price variability he encountered because prices were being established while trades were being made. One information science student said that she had not previously appreciated how critically important a strong infrastructure is for a successful trading desk. An economics major was struck by how the demand and supply analysis of microeconomics was working in our simulated equity market. Particularly memorable were the words of a young college student: "I really learned something," the student said. "What is it?" we inquired. "That I could never be a trader," the student replied.

Aim of This Book

As we have said, it is not only prospective traders whom we are addressing. Our objective is to help a far broader spectrum of people better appreciate the challenge of efficiently implementing portfolio decisions and discovering stock prices through trading. It is when you go to the market to trade that you realize how critically important finding liquidity is. It is when you see how your orders are handled and turned into trades that you will more fully appreciate that market structure and regulation matters.

These topics need to be understood, not just by prospective traders, but by a broad spectrum of other people. Of course, portfolio managers must understand the challenges their traders face and the order handling decisions they must make. CEOs, CFOs, and other high-level corporate managers should comprehend the dynamics of stock price formation and how these forces affect their share valuations and thus their company evaluations. Government regulators must comprehend the intricacies of the equity markets they are regulating. Journalists and communication professionals must understand the market's dynamics to better convey their views to the public. And, as you will see in Chap. 4, information science professionals also need to be informed in order to develop and maintain the necessary infrastructure for the technology-intense equity markets.

So, we welcome you to our book. Hopefully, it will help you cross the bridge that takes you from important academic materials to a real-world financial market.

Montclair, NJ, USA — Deniz Ozenbas
Villanova, PA, USA — Michael S. Pagano
New York, NY, USA — Robert A. Schwartz
Newark, DE, USA — Bruce W. Weber

Acknowledgment

For the production of this book, we are grateful for the assistance of Eileen Stempel, and for the support provided by the Robert A. Schwartz Center for Trading and Financial Markets Research. Link:

Robert A. Schwartz Center For Trading and Financial Markets Research - Zicklin School of Business | Baruch College (cuny.edu)

Contents

Economics and the Equity Market: A Microeconomics Course Application

1

Economics encompasses two broad subjects: macroeconomics and microeconomics. Macroeconomics deals with an economy in aggregate and addresses issues such as inflation, unemployment, interest rates, and economic growth. We present a macroeconomic perspective in Chap. 3. Microeconomics, the focus of this chapter, operates, as its name indicates, on the micro level, addressing household consumption decisions and the production decisions of firms. In this chapter, we focus on the parallels (and a few differences) between a standard microeconomics formulation (a household's selection of an optimal consumption bundle) and a standard finance model (an investor's selection of a portfolio that optimally combines a riskless asset – cash – and a risky equity portfolio). The finance formulation is the *Capital Asset Pricing Model (CAPM)*. CAPM is a keystone of what is known as modern portfolio theory, the originator of which is Harry Markowitz who was awarded a Nobel Memorial Prize in Economic Sciences in 1990 for having developed the theory of portfolio choice.

In both formulations, price plays a central role as it guides the decisions of both households and investors. Along with the decisions of households and firms, determination of an *equilibrium price* is of paramount importance. The price variable is so important that microeconomics courses can carry and have carried the name "price theory."

It is one thing to analyze price equilibrium in a theoretical model, and something else for an equilibrium price to actually be attained in a real-world market, especially one where prices are changing with great frequency, as is the case in an equity market. A primary function of a financial marketplace such as the New York Stock Exchange or Nasdaq is to facilitate attainment of equilibrium prices, an objective referred to as *price discovery*. Effective price discovery, however, is not easily achieved. We discuss this in considerably more detail in Chap. 2 (Finance) and in Chap. 3 (Macroeconomics).

For most of our discussion in this chapter, we assume, as is standard in much microeconomics, that the marketplace is a totally frictionless environment. By *frictionless*, we mean that there are no fees, taxes, or other impediments to buying and

D. Ozenbas et al., *Liquidity, Markets and Trading in Action*, Classroom Companion: Business, https://doi.org/10.1007/978-3-030-74817-3_1

selling, which, therefore, are costless activities. Only toward the end of the chapter do we relax this assumption and consider the impact that friction can have on price determination and the operations of a real-world equity market.

While a theoretical, frictionless market equilibrium might not be fully achieved in a real-world marketplace, an unobservable equilibrium price nevertheless exerts a force that improves the quality of market outcomes. This force merits being understood. By way of analogy, one might think of the power of the Gulf Stream, a strong, deep sea ocean current that brings warm water into the Atlantic Ocean from the Gulf of Mexico, moves up the Atlantic coast, and branches out to Europe. A ship crossing the Atlantic should take account of the Gulf Stream, but the vessel also has to contend with the winds, waves, and storms on the surface of the sea. One might equate the power of the Gulf Stream with the force exerted by an unobservable frictionless market equilibrium price and equate the wind, waves, and storms with frictions that buffet real-world, non-frictionless markets.

1.1 Microeconomics in a Nutshell

The terms *optimum, maximum*, and *equilibrium* play a key role in microeconomic analysis. Households are assumed to make "optimal" decisions when confronted by something that lies at the heart of a microeconomic problem: resolving a trade-off between alternative possibilities (e.g., get a little more of this and a little less of that, or vice versa). Optimality is achieved with regard to the decision maker's single, ultimate goal – maximize his/her personal utility. In a two-good environment (X and Y, for simplicity), a household determines the optimal amount of X to buy relative to Y when, because of a resource constraint (income or wealth), more of X can be obtained if and only if less of Y is obtained, and vice versa (more Y and less X). Having allocated its scarce resources optimally and, in so doing, having maximized utility, a household is in equilibrium.

A firm makes two optimal decisions in order to achieve a single goal – the maximization of profits. In a two-input environment (again, we are keeping it simple), a firm maximizes profits by (1) optimally combining L (let us call it labor) and C (let us call it physical capital) and (2) producing an optimal quantity of its product (let us stay with X). When a firm has done this, it too is in equilibrium.

A household's utility maximizing decisions are made with respect to tastes, income, and the prices of X and Y. An X-producing firm's profit maximizing decisions are made with respect to technology, the price of the product it is producing (the price of X), and the prices of its factors of production (L and C). When numerous households are consuming X, when many firms are producing X, and when all households and all firms are in equilibrium, the market for X is in equilibrium. We can obtain this equilibrium with the use of a downward sloping market demand curve to consume X and an upward sloping market supply curve to produce X.[1] The

[1] Intuitively stated, a price decrease attracts buyers to buy more, and a price increase attracts sellers to supply more.

intersection between these two curves identifies the equilibrium price of X and the quantity of X produced and consumed.

Note the critical role played by the prices of X, Y, L, and C in enabling households and firms to achieve equilibrium. As we have already noted, price is a key variable in microeconomics. The price of X, for instance, is a guiding light since it signals what has to be given up in return for more X. Because we have assumed that many individuals consume X and that many firms produce X, we take the market for X to be *perfectly competitive*. Accordingly, no participant, on either the demand or the supply side, is big enough to individually affect the price of X. Thus, all participants, both households and firms, are *price takers*, and the price that each one of them faces is determined by all participants as they meet collectively in the marketplace for X.

1.2 Microeconomic Analysis Goes to an Equity Market

Now let X be a share of stock, and take a microeconomics journey to an equity market to see how optimal investment decisions are made and how a stock's share price is determined. Following standard microeconomic methodology, we start by making assumptions that let us get answers that we are looking for while keeping the analysis as simple as possible. Here is our first assumption: the equity market is frictionless. Our second assumption is that, as with the consumer choice model, all investors are small, retail customers, and they are sizable enough in number so that no one of them has the power to individually affect the price of shares. Thus, the market is perfectly competitive, and all participants are price takers.

Like the highly simplified two-good consumer choice analysis of households, our treatment of the equity market deals with the optimal allocation of scarce financial resources between, not two goods, but two assets: a risky stock portfolio and cash (the riskless asset). Should the investor hold more stock and less cash or more cash and less stock? Like the consumer, the investor makes this allocation decision with reference to one goal: maximize expected personal utility. Why "expected utility," not just "utility"? For a simple reason. With the introduction of a risky asset, we are operating in an uncertain environment where the outcome is unknown.

As in the simplified two-good consumer model, allocation in the two-asset investment model is made with reference to the decision maker's tastes. But it is not taste or a preference for stock versus cash per se that matters. It is taste for two attributes of a financial asset: risk and return. For cash, risk is zero and the return is low; for a stock portfolio, there is risk and the return is higher. By substituting stock for cash, the investor increases his/her expected return and accepts more risk; by substituting cash for stock, the investor decreases his/her expected return and incurs less risk. The allocation decision is made with regard to this risk, return trade-off.

Exhibit 1.1 Indifference curve: a good versus good trade-off

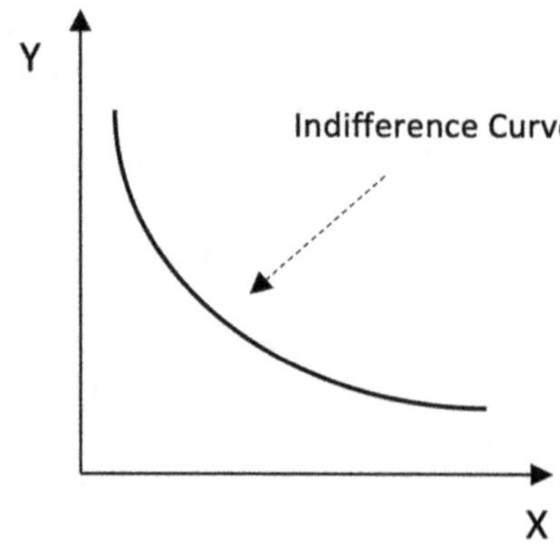

In the two-good consumer model, X and Y both deliver utility, and thus we have a "good versus good" trade-off. In the two-asset model, positive returns deliver increased utility, but investors are risk averse and so risk delivers "disutility" (i.e., a decrease in utility). Accordingly, with regard to the financial assets, we are dealing with a "good versus bad" trade-off.

1.3 Risk, Return Indifference Curves

Exhibit 1.1 displays a key microeconomics tool, an *indifference curve*, to depict a consumer's tastes for a good versus good trade-off. Because an indifference curve is the locus of points that deliver the same utility and because X and Y both yield positive utility, the indifference curve is downward sloping (it is also convex to the origin). All consumption combinations above and to the right of the indifference curve shown in Exhibit 1.1 yield more utility than combinations on the indifference curve, and all combinations below and to the left yield less. Accordingly, any X, Y combination above and to the right of the curve shown in Exhibit 1.1 lies on a higher indifference curve, and any X, Y combination below and to the left lies on a lower indifference curve.

Exhibit 1.2 presents an indifference curve that depicts an investor's tastes for a good versus bad trade-off. Here, the axes are labeled, respectively, risk and return. The properties of the curve shown in Exhibit 1.2 are the same as those shown in Exhibit 1.1 with one exception: the curve in Exhibit 1.2 is upward sloping. Why? Because investors are risk averse, they view risk as a bad. So if you get more risk, you also must get more return to stay on the same indifference curve.

Exhibit 1.2 Indifference curve: a good versus bad trade-off

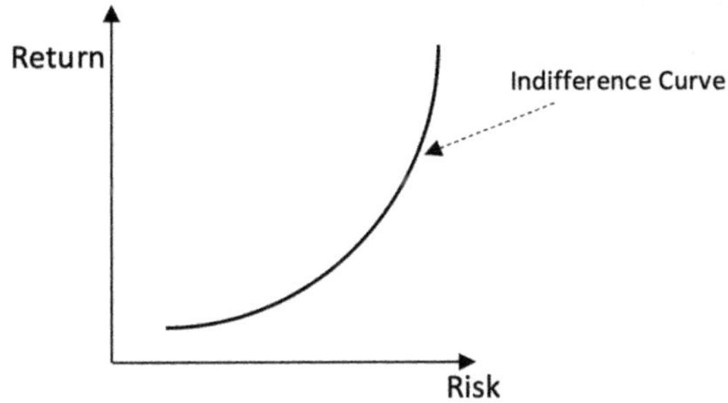

1.4 The Constraint

More structure is required for an optimal solution to be obtained. Specifically, a constraint is needed and, for the consumer, there is a constraint because income and wealth are scarce resources (for the investor, the situation is a bit different and we get to it shortly). For the consumer, the resource constraint is called a *budget constraint*. Let us take a look. Denote the consumer's income by M, and let M be allocated entirely to X and Y. Letting Y be the quantity of Y and X be the quantity of X, we have

$$M = P_Y Y + P_X X \tag{1.1}$$

Rearranging gives

$$Y = \frac{M}{P_Y} - \left(\frac{P_X}{P_Y}\right) X \tag{1.2}$$

Equation 1.2 is the budget constraint. We show it along with the indifference curve in Exhibit 1.3.

In Exhibit 1.3, a dot marks the point where the indifference curve is tangent to the budget constraint. The point of tangency marks the spot where the highest indifference curve (and thus the highest level of utility) can be reached (any other point along the budget constraint lies on a lower indifference curve). Accordingly, the point of tangency identifies the optimal (utility maximizing) combination of X and Y to consume.

The constraint is not as readily obtained for the investor as it is for the consumer. Instead of being determined by income and relative prices, the constraint depends on the risk-free rate for cash and on the risk and return combinations that are available. Regarding the risky component, are we dealing with one stock or with a portfolio of stocks? The answer is both. We first focus on the set of risky stocks and see how they can all be brought together to form one risky portfolio that includes all

Exhibit 1.3 Indifference curve and budget constraint

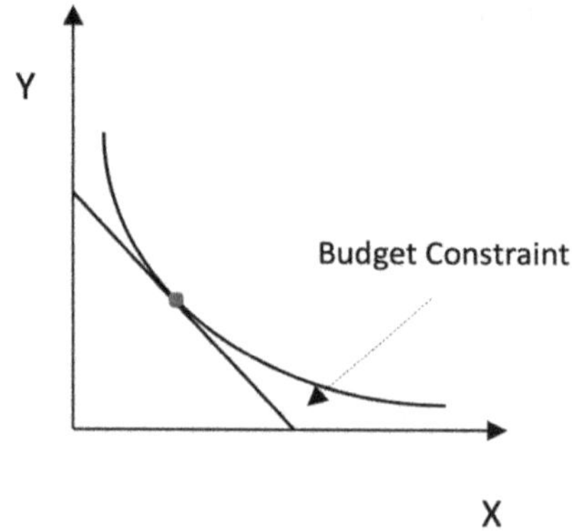

Exhibit 1.4 The efficient frontier

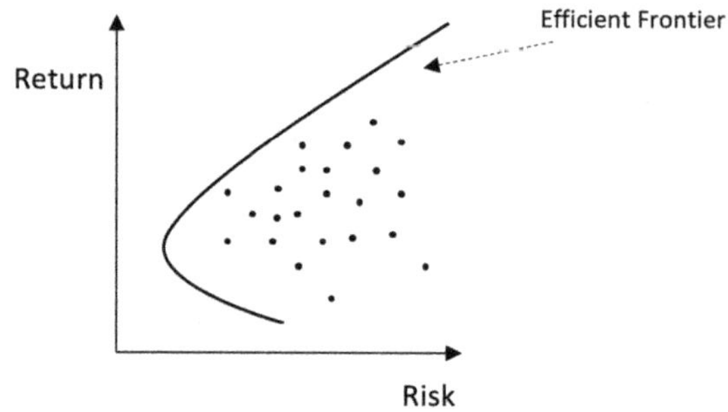

stocks. This all-inclusive portfolio is called the *market portfolio.*[2] Each stock's expected return, its standard deviation, and its covariance with the returns of other risky stocks are what we need to do this.[3] As we proceed, for the moment, let us keep cash to the side.

We can assess risk and return for all single-stock and multi-stock portfolios, with risk measured by the standard deviation of returns and expected return defined as the expected percentage price change for an individual stock and for a stock portfolio. Exhibit 1.4 shows a set of arbitrarily selected dots that represents a risk, return mapping for single-stock and multi-stock portfolios. The curve to the left of the dots is an outer envelope that shows the stock or stock portfolio for which the standard deviation is the lowest for any given return. The upward sloping, concave portion of the envelope, which also shows the maximum return that can be obtained for any given level of risk, is the *efficient frontier*. Portfolios that are inside the efficient frontier are inefficient because a higher expected return is available for each level of

---

[2]As we discuss in more detail below, this market portfolio should include all risky assets. In practice, the market portfolio is usually represented by a broad-based index such as the SP500.

[3]In finance, we typically use standard deviation as a measure of risk because it measures the dispersion around an average, or expected, rate of return on an asset.

Covariance (or its statistical cousin, correlation) measures how closely one stock's returns move in tandem with another stock's returns.

risk and, equivalently, a lower risk is available for each level of expected return. Only portfolios on the efficient frontier maximize return for a risk and minimize risk for a return, which explains why the curve is called the efficient frontier.

There is more; we are not there yet. We have not taken account of cash, the risk-free asset. This is how to proceed. The expected return on the investor's portfolio, $E(R_p)$, is

$$E(R_p) = (1-k) \cdot R_f + k \cdot E(R_m) \tag{1.3}$$

where k (a weight) is the percentage invested in the risky portfolio, R_f is the risk-free rate, and $E(R_m)$ is the expected return on the market portfolio. SD_p, the standard deviation of returns for a portfolio that contains both a risky stock portfolio and cash, is[4]

$$SD_p = k \cdot SD_m \tag{1.4}$$

where SD_m is the standard deviation of returns for the market portfolio. From Eq. 1.4, we have $k = SD_p/SD_m$. Substituting for k into 1.3 and rearranging gives

$$E(R_p) = R_f + \left[\frac{E(R_m) - R_f}{SD_m}\right] SD_p \tag{1.5}$$

What specific portfolio on the efficient frontier should be held in combination with cash? As before, the objective is to identify a portfolio that offers the highest expected return for any level of risk (measured by the standard deviation, SD) or, equivalently, that minimizes SD for any level of expected return. Two upward sloping lines are displayed in Exhibit 1.5. Both lines have the same intercept, R_f, and both pass through a portfolio on the efficient frontier. But one line crosses through

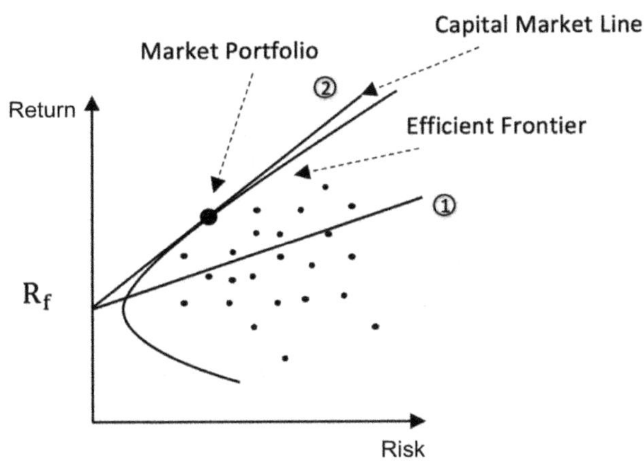

Exhibit 1.5 The capital market line

[4]With regard to Eq. 1.4, keep in mind that for cash (the risk-free asset), SD = 0. Thus, from $R_P = kR_m + (1-k)R_{cash}$, taking variances, we have $Var(R_p) = k^2 Var(R_m)$, from which Eq. 1.4 follows.

the efficient frontier, while the other is tangent to the efficient frontier. Which one of the two do you think is preferable? Answer: the line that is tangent dominates because, being steeper, it maximizes the expected return for each level of risk and, equivalently, it minimizes risk for each expected return.

Now go back to the flatter line in Exhibit 1.5 and picture rotating it counterclockwise with its intercept fixed at R_f. As it is rotated counterclockwise, it offers increasingly better risk, return combinations until it becomes tangent to the efficient frontier, at which point its slope is maximized. Thus, the line that is tangent is the one that we want. It is equivalent to the budget constraint shown in Exhibit 1.3. We call this line the *Capital Market Line*. The line forms the basis of a widely used financial model that is commonly referred to as the Capital Asset Pricing Model (CAPM). The portfolio that is on the efficient frontier at the point of tangency with the Capital Market Line is the *market portfolio.* We can now understand Eq. 1.5 as depicting the Capital Market Line. As noted earlier, the market portfolio should include all risky assets in the world but is usually represented by a large set of US stocks such as the S&P 500 stock index.

Unlike the budget constraint in the consumer choice model that varies from individual to individual according to his/her income and wealth, the Capital Market Line is the same for every investor, and so too is the market portfolio. But investors' tastes for risk vs. return differ from person to person, and each, with reference to his/her own indifference curves, selects the utility maximizing combination of the market portfolio and the risk-free asset. Where would the utility maximizing combination lie? It lies at the point where the investor's indifference curve is tangent to the Capital Market Line, as shown in Exhibit 1.6. Exhibit 1.7 contrasts the optimality solutions for two individuals with different tastes for risk and return.

Notice in Exhibit 1.6 that the indifference curve's point of tangency is to the left and below the Capital Market Line's point of tangency with the efficient frontier. This means that a relatively risk-averse individual will hold long positions in both cash and the market portfolio (i.e., the weight k will be less than 1). What if the indifference curve's point of tangency is to the right and above the Capital Market Line's point of tangency with the efficient frontier? In this case, the *less* risk-averse investor would borrow cash and invest a larger amount in the market portfolio (i.e.,

Exhibit 1.6 Investor optimality

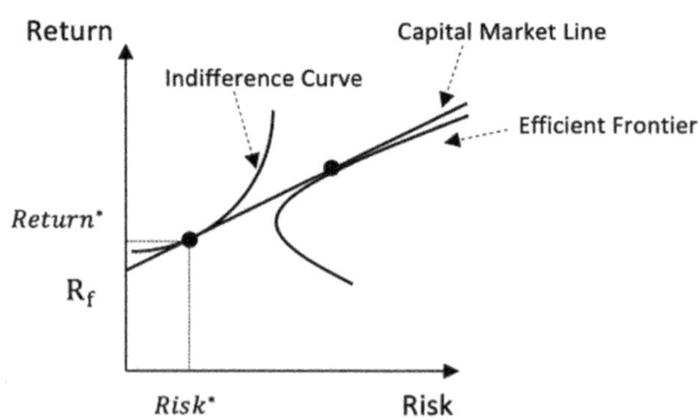

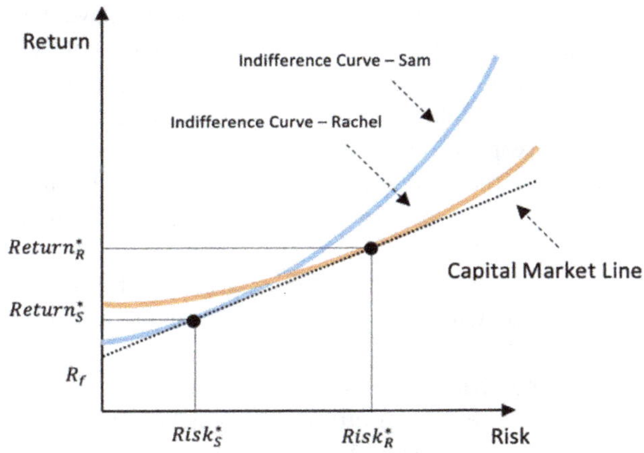

Exhibit 1.7 Optimality solution for two different investors

the weight, k, will be greater than 1). We discuss the weight later in this chapter with respect to Eq. 1.9.

There we have it! This is how an investor's risk, return trade-off is resolved. To illustrate, consider two investors with indifference curves that are different. Sam will accept additional risk but only for a substantial increase in expected return. Rachel, on the other hand, will tolerate added risk for smaller improvements in expect return. Rachel's optimal portfolio is riskier than Sam's.

1.5 Demand Curve to Hold Shares of the Market Portfolio

Thus far, we see that the investment model closely parallels the standard consumer choice model. Now for the next, more advanced step. From indifference curves and budget constraints, we can obtain demand curves for the goods and services that households consume. From our risk, return analysis, are we able to obtain a downward sloping demand curve to hold shares of the market portfolio and of individual stocks?

For an individual stock, the answer in a frictionless, perfectly liquid environment is simple. Investors do not have tastes for the individual stocks themselves – all that matters to them is risk and return. In the Capital Asset Pricing Model, risk is measured by the beta coefficient, and two stocks or portfolio of stocks that have the same beta coefficient are perfect substitutes for each other.[5] As such, they should be

[5] A beta coefficient (β) is an estimate of a stock's riskiness relative to the riskiness of the market portfolio (R_m).

Beta is a measure of systematic risk. Risk that refers to that component of a stock's return that is not related to the market return is referred to as non-systematic risk. Non-systematic risk is not priced because, in the frictionless environment, it can be eliminated by portfolio diversification (whereas systematic risk cannot be eliminated by diversification).

priced to yield the same expected return. And all stocks do have perfect substitutes because the risk of any stock can be replicated by an appropriately weighted combination of two other stocks. Because all stocks have perfect substitutes, the demand curve for each stock is horizontal (and thus infinitely elastic) at a price $P_{m0} = a$ that we explain below with respect to Eq. 1.6.

The demand curve for the market portfolio, however, is downward sloping. To obtain it requires analysis, and to this end, we first set forth our assumptions.

1. There are two financial assets: cash and the market portfolio.
2. A single holding period with a starting point in time denoted by 0 and an ending point in time denoted by T.
3. At point in time 0, the investor is holding only cash.
4. The investor maximizes expected utility given his/her initial cash holdings, the risk-free rate (R_f), risk, and $E(P_{mT})$ which is the expected price of the market portfolio at point in time T.
5. $E(P_{mT})$ is independent of P_{m0}, the price of the market portfolio at point in time 0.
6. The environment is frictionless. There are no commissions, borrowing costs, short-sale restrictions, etc.

With these assumptions, we can obtain the investor's demand curve to hold shares of the market portfolio. The demand curve, presented with the price P_{m0} on the left-hand side, is the linear equation:[6]

$$P_{m0} = a - 2b \cdot N \tag{1.6}$$

where

- N is the number of shares of the market portfolio purchased and held
- $a = E(P_{mT})/(1 + R_f)$ is the intercept parameter
- $b = \pi/(1 + R_f)$ is the slope parameter
- π is a risk premium that reflects the investor's risk aversion[7]

This demand curve is shown in Exhibit 1.8. Several things are of interest regarding this demand curve:

1. The consumption of most goods is measured as a rate per a period of time, for instance, the amount of X consumed per day, per month, or per year. This is not the case for financial assets, for they are not "consumed" over time. Rather, they are "held," and the demand curve shows that the number of shares held depends on the price of shares.

[6] The derivation is in Ho, Schwartz, and Whitcomb (1985), and further discussion is provided in Francioni, Hazarika, Reck, and Schwartz (2010).

[7] The risk premium is the compensation required for an investor to hold a risky asset instead of a riskless asset (cash).

Exhibit 1.8 Demand to hold shares of the market portfolio

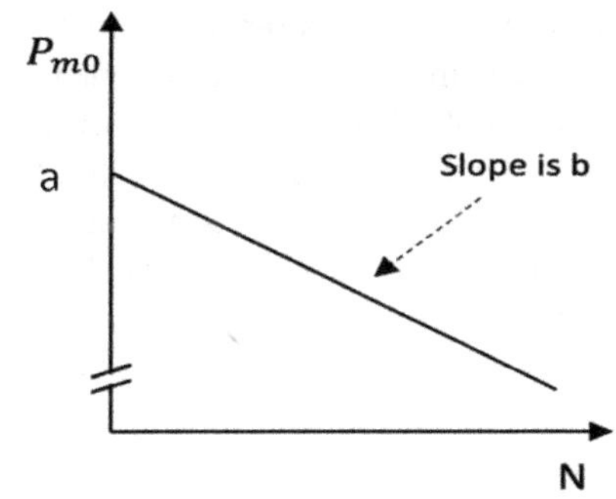

2. Assumption 5 indicates that $E(P_{mT})$, a term in the expression for the intercept parameter, is independent of P_{m0}, the price of the market portfolio at point in time 0. By this assumption, we ignore the unnecessary complexity of the price intercept being related to the price at which transactions are made, which would be the case if price conveyed an informational signal. With independence, as the current price of the market portfolio decreases while $E(P_{mT})$ is constant, the expected return over the holding period rises. Or let us state it this way: if the current price goes down and the expected future price stays constant, the expected return must go up.
3. The demand curve described by Eq. 1.6 and shown in Exhibit 1.8 is linear. Linearity is desirable because it is a good deal easier to work with. Note that price is on the left-hand side of Eq. 1.6, not its usual location on the right-hand side of a demand equation. We have switched the side simply to obtain linearity. To achieve linearity, one further assumption is required: that shares are priced such that the difference between the return on the market portfolio and the risk-free rate is small enough to ignore.[8] In other words, we have to remain in the area of the demand curve that is reasonably close to the price intercept. This certainly makes sense. With linearity throughout, the demand curve would intersect the quantity axis, at which point a finite number of shares would be held at a price of zero. This would not make sense. If shares were free, they should be held in unlimited amounts, and thus, the demand curve must become curvilinear as the price approaches zero in order to capture this behavior.[9]
4. The slope of the negatively inclined demand curve reflects the investor's risk premium parameter, π. The more risk averse the investor, the greater is the slope. If the investor is risk neutral rather than risk averse), the slope, b, would be zero, and the demand curve would be horizontal (infinitely elastic) at the price intercept, a. Why? Because, with risk neutrality, the risky asset and the risk-free asset are perfect substitutes.

[8] This assumption is explained in further detail in Ho, Schwartz, and Whitcomb (1985).

[9] As the price becomes asymptotically close to zero, the number of shares demanded, N, would increase without bound. So a linear relationship is not possible for all price points.

5. The intercept parameter, a, contains the term, $E(P_{mT})$. As we discuss in some detail in Chapter 2, different investors can have different (divergent) expectations of this end-of-period price, and thus, the location of the demand curve will differ from investor to investor. In consumer choice theory, the demand curve for good X differs from consumer to consumer because of differences in their tastes for the product and their wealth. For the risky asset, demand differs among investors because of differences in their taste (really, distaste) for risk and/or their expectations of future returns.

Equation (1.6) contains a number of parameters. Juggling them around, we can obtain the following equation:[10]

$$\frac{\pi'}{P_{m0}} = E(R_m) - R_f \tag{1.7}$$

where π' is the investor's marginal risk premium and, because of the division by P_{m0}, the left-hand side, like the right-hand side, has a percentage dimension. Equation 1.7 has an interesting interpretation, one that is equivalent to that of the consumer choice model. In the consumer choice model, at the point where the consumer's indifference curve is tangent to his/her budget constraint, we have

$$\frac{Marginal\ Utility\ of\ X}{Marginal\ Utility\ of\ Y} = \frac{Price\ of\ X}{Price\ of\ Y} \tag{1.8}$$

Equation 1.8 says that when the consumer has allocated his/her resources optimally, the rate at which he/she can substitute X for Y while keeping utility constant (the left-hand side of the equation) equals the rate at which X can be substituted for Y in the marketplace keeping total expenditures constant (the right-hand side of the equation). Thus, we see that the consumer harmonizes his/her tastes, on the margin, with the trade-off that is possible in the marketplace.

Equivalently, for the CAPM, at the point where the investor's indifference curve is tangent to the Capital Market Line (refer to Exhibit 1.6), the investor's marginal risk premium expressed as a percent of price (refer to Eq. 1.7) equals $(E(R_m) - R_f)$, which is the higher percentage return that the market offers the investor for accepting risk rather than holding cash. To understand this intuitively, think of the risk premium as a price: the price that the market will pay the investor for accepting risk. To repeat, we see that, in a frictionless world, the decision maker maximizes his/her expected utility by harmonizing his/her own tastes (on the margin) with the price of risk, which can be understood as the rate at which two inputs into utility (risk and return) can be substituted for each other in the market.

So this is what we have. In the consumer choice model, the rate at which X can be substituted for Y is the price of X relative to the price of Y. In CAPM, the rate at which risk can be substituted for certainty equals the risk premium that the market offers. In both the consumer choice model and CAPM, the decision maker

[10] Further discussion and its derivation are provided in Schwartz (1991) and in Francioni, Hazarika, Reck, and Schwartz (2010).

maximizes utility by harmonizing his/her utility trade-off (the left hand side of Eq. 1.7) with the trade-off that is possible in the market (the right hand side of Eq. 1.7).

By further juggling the parameters in Eq. (1.6), we can obtain[11]

$$W = \frac{E(Rm) - r_f}{Var\left(r_m\right) R_R} \tag{1.9}$$

where W is an investor's weight in the market portfolio and R_R is a measure of his/her risk aversion. The equation makes intuitive sense: an investor's optimal weight in the risky market portfolio is greater (all else equal) the greater is the risk premium, $[E(R_m) - R_f]$, the less risky is the market portfolio $[\mathrm{Var}(r_m)]$, and the less risk averse is the investor (the smaller is his/her R_R). Note that the only term in Eq. 1.9 that is specific to an investor is the risk aversion parameter, R_R.

Regarding the distribution of the weight W across investors, a participant with a relatively high R_R and $W < 1$ will have a long position in both cash and the risky market portfolio, while a participant with $W = 1$ will be neither a borrower nor a lender, and a participant with a relatively low R_R and $W > 1$ will borrow at the risk-free rate (i.e., acquire a short position in cash) so as to finance his/her leveraged long position in the risky market portfolio. Now, consider the dynamics that come into play when the long positions in cash of the $W < 1$ investors are the source of lending to the $W > 1$ investors. To this end, let us ask: how is equilibrium between the long and the short cash positions achieved when, to repeat, the long cash positions of some investors finance other investors' leveraged long positions in the market portfolio?

The total amount borrowed by $W > 1$ investors is brought into line with the total amount lent by $W < 1$ investors by an equilibrating variable which, consistent with standard microeconomics theory, is a price. The price is the risk premium, $E(R_m) - R_f$. In analyzing how the risk premium fulfills this role, let us for simplicity treat R_f as an exogenously determined constant so that the risk premium changes only with $E(R_m)$.[12] Note that the relative aggressiveness of the $W > 1$ investors exerts upward pressure on the share price of the market portfolio and, in so doing, decreases $E(R_m)$, while the relative nonaggressiveness of the $W < 1$ investors exerts downward pressure on the share price of the market portfolio and, in so doing, increases $E(R_m)$. When the upward and downward pressures are in balance, equilibrium has been achieved. In equilibrium, $E(R_m)$ and the risk premium would be at a level where the amount of cash borrowed by $W > 1$ investors just equals the amount that $W < 1$ investors desire to lend.

[11] As noted above, further discussion and the equation's derivation are provided in Schwartz (1991) and in Francioni, Hazarika, Reck, and Schwartz (2010).

[12] In the financial markets, R_f is not determined by the balance between borrowing and lending in the equity markets alone. Other financial markets and the Federal Reserve Bank's macroeconomic policy are also major determinants of R_f. Regardless, we could obtain an equivalent result by holding $E(R_m)$ and allowing R_f to vary, rising when the demand for cash exceeds its supply, and falling when the supply of cash exceeds its demand.

1.6 What About the Supply Curve?

On to the next question. After we aggregate individual investor demand curves to get a market demand curve, how do we obtain the equilibrium price and number of shares of the market portfolio that each investor will hold? With regard to consumer choice analysis, we would do this by obtaining a supply curve to match against the demand curve to get an equilibrium solution. Can we now obtain a meaningful supply curve for shares?

One candidate for the supply curve that might come to mind is to take account of the number of shares of the market portfolio that are outstanding. To do this, we would aggregate the individual demand curves depicted in Exhibit 1.8 and match the aggregate with a vertical line located on the horizontal axis at the number of shares outstanding. Could this vertical line be the supply curve? We answer this question by considering what would happen if the number of shares outstanding is changed so that the location of the "supply curve" shifts. Say, the company splits its shares 2 for 1. Would this change the total value of shares outstanding? No, it would not. Following a 2 for 1 split, the price of shares would simply be cut in half. This being the case, what would the market's demand to hold shares look like? It would be a downward sloping, convex curve that satisfies the condition that at all points along the curve, price times the number of shares outstanding is a constant. In other words, the demand curve would be a rectangular hyperbola. Such a curve would be valueless. Thus, the vertical line cannot be considered a supply curve.

In point of fact, there is no supply curve to match with the demand curve. Think about it. There are no separate suppliers, as there are for the consumption goods X and Y in the consumer choice model. In the financial model, any participant can be either a buyer (demander) or a seller (supplier) of shares, depending on the price of shares. This being the case, how do we proceed so as to identify an equilibrium price?

1.7 Buy and Sell Curves

There is another route to follow. As we take it, we relax the assumption that the investor's starting position was 100% in cash and 0% in shares of the market portfolio. This assumption was not necessary for the analysis; we made it only to simplify the specification of the intercept and slope parameters, a and b.

Go back to the individual investor's demand curve shown in Exhibit 1.8 and draw in a vertical line at the number of shares of the market portfolio that the investor is currently holding, N_{m0}. Such a line is shown in Exhibit 1.9. Go to the price where the vertical line intersects the demand curve. At all higher prices, the investor wants to hold fewer shares than are currently in his/her portfolio, and at all lower prices, the investor wants to hold more shares. In effect, prices *above* P_{m0} will turn the investor into a *seller* of some of his/her shares, and prices *below* P_{m0} will cause the investor to be a *buyer* of more shares to add to his current holdings. We can use this insight to form buy and sell curves. To visualize this, direct your attention to Exhibit 1.9 and shift the price axis to the right, to where the vertical line is placed, so that part of the demand curve is in the negative quadrant. Flip that part of the demand curve over from the negative quadrant (where it is viewed as a negative buy) to the positive quadrant (where, without the minus sign, it is viewed as a positive sell). Relabel the upward sloping curve "Sell" and relabel the downward sloping portion "Buy," as we have done in Exhibit 1.9, and relabel the horizontal axis Q which we do, not in Exhibit 1.9, but in Exhibit 1.10 From the demand curve, we now have a positively inclined sell curve and a negatively inclined buy curve, with the two curves branching off the vertical line at the price where the vertical line at N_{mo} intersects the investor's demand curve.

Buy and sell curves of two investors are shown in Exhibit 1.10. This exhibit is related to Exhibit 1.9 except that the horizontal axis is labeled "Q" (for the number of shares bought or sold), not "N" (for the number of shares held). The buy/sell curves for the second market participant (which are labeled B2 and S2, respectively)

Exhibit 1.9 From the demand curve to buy and sell curves

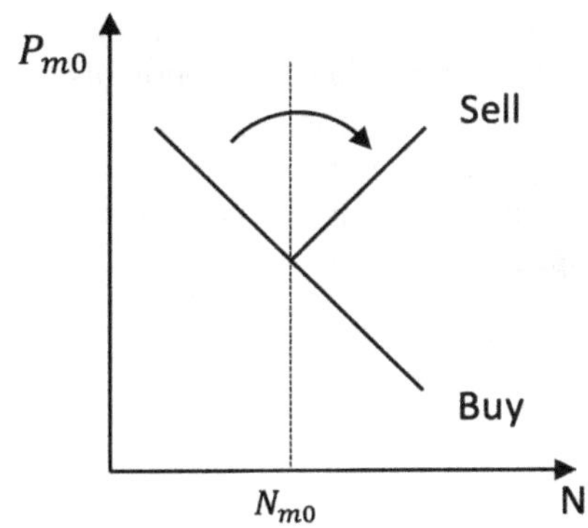

Exhibit 1.10 Buy and sell curves of two participants

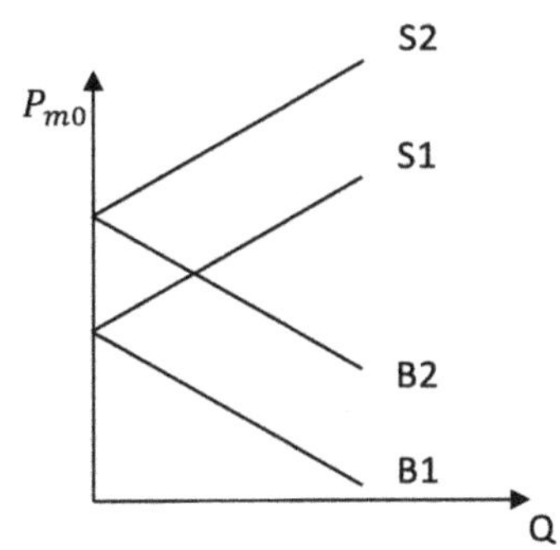

are higher than the curves for the first participant (which are labeled B1 and S1, respectively). Why do the buy/sell curves for the second participant have a higher price intercept than the buy/sell curves for the first participant? Either because initial share holdings are less for the second participant or because the second participant has a higher expectation of the end of period price, $E(P_{mT})$. Either way, his/her demand curve has a higher intercept on the price axis. Because the buy/sell curves are lower for the first participant than for the second, the upward sloping sell curve for the first participant intersects the downward sloping buy curve for the second participant. Accordingly, the first participant will sell shares at a price at which the second will buy, and thus, a trade can be made.

Now, let there be many buy/sell curves, all with different price intercepts. Aggregating these gives us the downward sloping market buy curve and the upward sloping market sell curve that are shown in Exhibit 1.11 (for simplicity, both curves are presented as linear). The upward sloping sell curve plays the role of a supply curve, but it is not what one might consider a traditional supply curve. In our setting, there is no traditional supply curve. There is a sell curve that can be matched with a buy curve, and this is all we need to obtain the equilibrium price of shares.

The equilibrium price, as shown in Exhibit 1.11, is set where the market buy and market sell curves intersect. Each participant buys or sells shares at this price and, in so doing, achieves an optimal cash-and-shares portfolio. Following the purchases and sales, each investor is holding the exact number of shares desired given the equilibrium price. At this point, there will be no follow-up trades. That is, there will be no desire on anyone's part to re-contract. The market is in equilibrium. This speaks to the efficiency of the perfectly efficient, perfectly liquid market. Let us label the frictionless market equilibrium price, P*, as shown in Exhibit 1.11, and the equilibrium number of shares traded is labeled Q*.

Exhibit 1.11 Market buy and sell curves

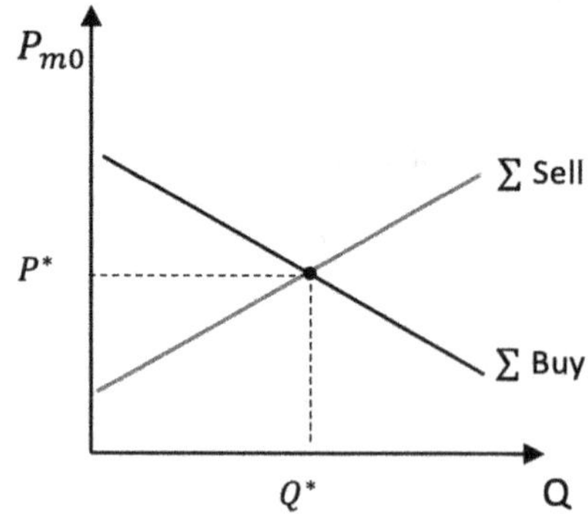

1.8 The Non-frictionless Market

What if the market is not frictionless? Will all trades still be made at the equilibrium price, P*? To answer this question, we introduce friction into the analysis.

There is one simple way to do this: do not allow participants to submit their full, continuous buy and sell curves. This constraint certainly is realistic. What would the response be if you were to contact your broker and, in placing an order, state the intercept and slope parameters of your buy/sell curves? The broker would certainly be confused and probably would think that you are a bit crazy! Of course, real-world investors like us do not do this. We simply state an order that stipulates a price and the number of shares to be bought or sold. This constraint is not at all equivalent to the imposition of a minimum or a maximum price limit. It is simply that the investor submits just one price and one number of shares to buy or to sell. Assume the selection is made optimally, given the participant's demand curve to hold shares and his/her expectation of what the clearing price will be.

While continuing to assume that the investor knows his/her complete buy and sell curves, we have introduced one basic reality of a non-frictionless market. Further, let us introduce a bit of market structure. This is something that is not germane to the frictionless world, but it is important when friction is introduced. Consider the order placement decisions of investors as they approach the 9:30 opening of an equity market such as the New York Stock Exchange or Nasdaq.

Before the market opens, no participant can know the equilibrium price of a stock, P*, but each has an expectation of what it might be. Each participant's strategic order placement decision is based on two determinants: (1) his/her expectation concerning P* and (2) the slope and intercept parameters of his/her own buy and sell curves.

Question: If all participants price and size their orders according to the above two determinants, will the market's opening price be P*?

Answer: Only by dumb luck! It would occur as a very special case that depends on the accuracy of investor expectations of P* and on how their buy/sell curves are distributed around P*.[13]

Conclusion: Our frictionless market gives a wonderfully efficient security market solution that one would expect from a microeconomic analysis of a perfectly competitive, perfectly liquid market. But the finding does not hold in a real-world financial market once friction is introduced.

---

[13] Ho, Schwartz, and Whitcomb (1985) provide further discussion and analysis.

1.9 Wrap Up: Microeconomics in a Non-frictionless Financial Market

This chapter is focused on the parallels between a household's selection of an optimal consumption bundle (product X and product Y) and an investor's selection of an optimal combination of the riskless asset (cash) and a risky asset (an equity portfolio). In our discussion, we first assume away all transaction costs and operate in a frictionless environment. Then, at the end of the chapter, we introduce friction by constraining the investor to submitting, not the complete, continuous buy and sell curves we used to identify an equilibrium price, but just one single-priced order that is optimally selected given the individual's complete buy and sell curves and his/her expectation of what the equilibrium price might be. Given this one real-world constraint, we have shown that market prices will generally deviate from perfectly competitive equilibrium values even in a market that comprises an unbounded number of order placers, each of whom is a price taker.

In the introduction to this chapter, we noted that an unobservable, frictionless market equilibrium price can exert its force on price determination in real-world markets even if realized transaction prices differ from equilibrium values. Think back to our analogy at the beginning of the chapter where we contrast the force of the deep-water Gulf Stream with the winds, waves, and storms that perturb the surface of the sea.

Like the winds, waves, and storms, a broad array of market frictions perturbs real-world financial market operations and price discovery. Consider the enormous difficulty of dealing with complex information sets that are huge, often imprecise, incomplete, inaccurate, and not equally shared by all. Recognize that investors can have divergent expectations based on publicly available information. Take a close look at trading costs such as bid-ask spreads, opportunity costs, and market impact costs. Understand why short-period (e.g., intraday) price volatility is sharply accentuated. Note the importance of the rules and regulations that define a market's structure. Appreciate the need for liquidity and the importance of achieving high-quality price discovery. We deal with all of this (and more) in the next chapter which turns to our finance course application.

Liquidity, Trading, and Price Determination in Equity Markets: A Finance Course Application

2

The relationship between fundamental information and the price of equity shares is critically important. Fundamental information encompasses a vast array of items that pertain to individual firms, to industries, and to the broad, macro economy. In investment courses, the relationship is considered with respect to portfolio formation. In corporate finance, the relationship is considered with respect to asset valuations and the determination of a firm's cost of capital.

The transformation of fundamental information into share prices starts with the information set and extends to investors (both individual and institutional) and then to the marketplace where equity shares are traded and share prices determined. In so doing, fundamental information is transformed into three factors: (1) expected future returns, (2) uncertainty concerning future returns (an investment's risk), and (3) the difficulty of buying and selling shares in the market (liquidity risk).

In broad brush, this is how it works. Assume that a stock's expected 1-year forward price is $55 a share. If shares are currently priced at $50, the expected return on the investment is 10%. If, concurrently, the risk-free rate of interest is 4%, the stock is priced to yield a 6% premium. What accounts for the premium? Two things: risk and illiquidity.

Risk exists because what a stock's actual price will be one year from now is unknown in the present. The stock's *expected* share price is $55. One year later, the price could turn out to be nicely higher than $55 or disappointingly lower. Thus, the investment is risky, and very importantly, investors are risk averse. Accordingly, the premium compensates them for accepting risk. But is that all it compensates investors for? No, investors are also averse to illiquidity.

Risk pertains to a future share value, while illiquidity matters when shares are bought or sold. Here is a simple, intuitive definition of what the term liquidity means: the ability to buy or to sell shares reasonably quickly, in reasonable amounts, and at reasonable prices. In a frictionless environment, the market would be perfectly liquid, trading would be costless, and shares could be bought or sold

D. Ozenbas et al., *Liquidity, Markets and Trading in Action*, Classroom Companion: Business, https://doi.org/10.1007/978-3-030-74817-3_2

instantly at an appropriate price. But equity markets are not frictionless,[1] trading is not at all costless (we explain more about this in Sect. 2.2), and transaction costs are higher the more illiquid a market is.

Let us back up for a moment. How are investors compensated for risk? By a risk premium. How are they compensated for buying shares that they know can be difficult to sell in the future? By an illiquidity premium. Accordingly, let us repeat: with the risk-free rate at 4%, buying shares at $50 while expecting a 1-year forward price of $55 yields a premium of 6%, and this premium compensates investors both for accepting risk and for bearing the cost of illiquidity.

So what is liquidity? As we have just said, a good intuitive definition of this slippery term is the ease with which shares can be traded. Can they be traded quickly? Can they be traded in reasonable quantity and at a reasonable price? If the answer is yes, yes, yes, then we can say that the market for a company's shares is liquid. But what benchmark might there be for assessing, for an order of a given number of shares, the time taken to fill it and the price at which the trade has been made? And can the assessments of time, price, and size be aggregated into a single quantitative measure of liquidity? They cannot, so where do we stand? Hang on, we return to a further discussion of liquidity in Sect. 2.7 of this chapter.

For most stocks, speed is not an issue in today's modern electronic markets. What about size? Size is not an issue for smaller, retail-sized orders, but it is a major challenge for institutional-sized orders (for instance, an order of 50,000 shares, 100,000 shares, or more). What about price? Have you observed how rapidly prices change in short, intraday intervals? They bounce around, often with such rapidity that you can look at a price one instant, blink, and then look again and the stock's share value has changed. Clearly, in this environment, trading at a "reasonable" price is difficult to accomplish, and it is not even easy to know what a reasonable price is.

One glance at a computer screen with "real-time" prices will convince you of this. At times, price rises (or falls) over a series of trades, turns direction, and then shoots back down (or up). What might explain this volatility? Finding prices that best reflect the broad market's desire to hold shares is complex and dynamic. The process is called *price discovery*. We pursue this thought further in Sect. 2.4 of this chapter.

Buying and selling shares is clearly not costless. Costs exist in the form of commissions and fees. They also exist for a participant who wants to consummate a trade quickly by buying or selling "at market" because there is a spread between the price at which one can buy shares (the lowest posted asking quote on the market) and the price at which one can sell shares (the highest posted bid quote on the market). The difference between the best buy and the best sell quotes is the *bid-ask*

[1] Friction is the total implicit and explicit costs associated with the execution of a financial transaction.

spread. The spread can be thought of as the cost of buying or selling with immediacy. Then, there is the cost big traders incur when their large buy orders push price up, or their large sell orders push price down. This is referred to as a *market impact cost*. There is also an opportunity cost. We identify and discuss these costs in Sect. 2.2.

And so buying and selling shares to implement a portfolio decision is not costless. The costs referred to in the previous paragraph exist because equity markets are not frictionless. The distinction between frictionless and non-frictionless markets is of tremendous importance. The notion of "frictionless" is in the same spirit as the concept of frictionless physics.[2] This contrasts markedly from a non-frictionless equity market where: 1) commissions are not zero, 2) there are fees and taxes, 3) trading with immediacy requires paying the bid-ask spread, and 4) buying a large number of shares can push price up, and selling a large number can push price down.

One reality is a root cause of much of the complexity that surrounds trading, liquidity creation, and price determination: investors commonly differ in their interpretations of the fundamental information that applies to specific stocks, industries, and the broad economy, and their differing interpretations translate into their having different expectations about what a stock's future price will be. We refer to this as *divergent expectations*. What are divergent expectations attributable to? Answer: information sets are of enormous size. Moreover, they are incomplete, replete with complexities, ambiguities, and inaccuracies (surprise, surprise). What is the effect of expectations being divergent? It accounts for:

- Discovering reasonable prices in a marketplace being a difficult, complex process
- Good trading being a challenging activity
- Prices being excessively volatile in brief intervals of time
- The design of equity market structure being of critical importance

The difference between homogeneous expectations and divergent expectation merits more attention. Here is how it works. As we have noted, market participants price their orders with regard to the future values that they expect their investments to deliver. Would a community of investors have identical expectations of future values (the means and variances of returns), or might their expectations differ? If their expectations are identical, we say that they have *homogeneous expectations*. If they differ, we say that investors have *divergent expectations*. The distinction is of major importance. Here is one reason why. If investors' expectations are homogeneous, shares can be thought of as having fundamental ("intrinsic") values that can be found by stock analysts. If investors' expectations are divergent, shares do not have fundamental values, and share prices must be found in the marketplace where trades are made. And price discovery is a major function of a stock exchange. What are

[2] As discussed in Chapter 1, some topics may be discussed initially assuming frictionless environments, and then friction is added to measure the impact.

your thoughts about this? What do you believe best describes investor expectations: homogeneous or divergent?

In this introductory section of the chapter, we have touched on an array of thoughts regarding information, risk, liquidity, trading costs, market structure, and their effects on price determination. Aside from business school students (and other interested people), who should understand these concepts? Of course, the list includes portfolio managers, traders, and the exchanges themselves, but these are not the only stakeholders. As we have noted in the Preface, also important are corporate CEOs and other corporate officials of publicly traded companies, information technology professionals who build and maintain trading systems, regulators who oversee the markets, business journalists, and the investing public.

2.1 Order Types

Recognizing that investors communicate with the market via the orders that they submit, we next turn our attention to two basic, plain vanilla types: market orders and limit orders.

A market order is an order to trade at the best available price, while a limit order specifies a price limit. For example, "buy 100 shares with a limit price of $50" means do not buy at any price greater than $50. Equivalently, "sell 100 shares at a limit price of $51" means do not sell at any price lower than $51. Limit orders provide liquidity to the market because once they are posted, they sit on the book waiting for a counterparty to submit a market order. Market orders are "liquidity-taking" because they execute quickly against whatever the current best posted price is on the book and, in so doing, they eliminate the liquidity-providing limit order from the book. Thus, limit orders are "makers" of liquidity, while market orders are "takers" of liquidity.

A limit order is passive because after it has been posted, the order simply sits on the book waiting for a willing counterparty to submit a market order. If a counterparty does not materialize, the order does not execute. Consequently, there is a risk that the limit order will not execute (which is referred to as *non-execution risk*). In contrast, this cost is not borne by the trader who uses a market order.

In addition to non-execution risk, while posted on a transparent limit order book, a limit order can be "picked off" following an unexpected advent of unfavorable information (if the limit order trader has not yet received the news and has not withdrawn the order in time). This (along with non-execution risk) is a cost that a limit order trader incurs that a market order trader does not incur. On the other hand, limit orders can execute at better prices than market orders because they save the bid-ask spread. Consequently, resolving these trade-offs and choosing between a limit order or a market order calls for some strategic decision-making.

Other special order types are also used. Some of the more popular ones are:

- A "stop order" is an order that becomes active only if a trade is made at or through the stop price. For example, "sell 100 shares stopped at $30, limit $29" means that once a trade has been made at $30 or below, the order is activated and displayed on the book with a limit price of $29.

- "Discretionary, not-held orders" give the broker the freedom to make the execution at any time and at a price that is fit and reasonable, given the investor's goals. "Not-held" means that the broker is "not held responsible" if an attempt to get a better price fails and the order is eventually executed at an inferior price.
- "Pegged orders" are orders where the limit price is pegged to a benchmark such as the NBB (national best bid), the NBO (national best offer), or the midpoint of the two, and thus, the limit price changes as the benchmark price changes.
- "Iceberg orders" reveal only a small portion of the full order. Once the small, revealed portion of an iceberg order is executed, another small portion is posted on the book and displayed to the market.

Orders can also have special conditions attached to them. Two common ones are:

- Fill or kill (if the order cannot be filled upon arrival, cancel it)
- All or nothing (if the order cannot be filled in its entirety, do not fill it at all)

In today's markets, more traders are relying heavily on algorithmic trading (also called algo trading or computerized trading) to enter their orders. Algo trading is based on computer programs that follow defined decision rules (algorithms) to generate and submit orders. Algorithmic trading typically operates at speeds that are impossible for a human trader to match (e.g., milliseconds). Nevertheless, a human participant must still design an algo and decide when to activate it.

For three reasons, some orders are not revealed to the market, and some are not even transmitted to a trading facility.

1. An exchange's limit order book can only accept orders conditioned on price alone. The reason for this is that orders on the book must be subject to aggregation so that the total number of shares at a price can be unequivocally stated. Orders with special conditions (such as fill or kill) cannot be aggregated, are therefore kept separate, and are not disclosed.
2. Large traders do not want to reveal the full size of their orders because displaying this information will cause an undue market impact.
3. Participants who handle their orders strategically find it effective to enter an order only when they feel that the conditions are favorable for doing so.

The unrevealed (hidden) orders and the liquidity they provide are called *latent*. The latent orders translate into latent liquidity.

2.2 Trading Costs

Trading is a complex process because it is not costless. Let us take a closer look at what the costs are.

Trading costs fall into two categories: *explicit* and *implicit*. Explicit costs are visible and easily measured. They include commissions, fees, and taxes. Implicit costs are trickier to measure. They include the bid-ask spread that was described earlier, opportunity costs, and market impact.

Bid-ask spreads are a natural property of a continuous market. Bid and ask prices are established by limit order traders and/or by market makers. Because matched and crossed orders trigger transactions that eliminate them from the book, market bid-ask spreads are always positive. Further, with discrete prices, the spread must be at least as large as the smallest allowable price variation (currently one cent for stocks in the United States). Market order traders buy at the ask and sell at the bid, and for them, the bid-ask spread is the cost of a round trip (buying and then selling, or selling short and then buying).[3]

Opportunity costs are incurred when a trader is not able to complete a trade or when there are execution delays. This cost is particularly relevant for limit order traders. A limit order buyer incurs an opportunity cost if a stock's price rises and his/her limit order, because it was priced too low, remains unexecuted on the book. A seller similarly incurs this cost if a stock's price declines and his/her limit order to sell, because it was priced too high, remains unexecuted on the book.

Market impact (also referred to as "price impact") is encountered by large traders. For one thing, a large order sent as a single block to the market can "walk the book." That is, it can execute in part at the best counterpart bid or offer, and after it has cleared out the shares at the best price, it moves to the next price rung on the ladder (higher if it is a buy order and further down if it is a sell order), and so on. Or if the large order is brought to market in smaller pieces over an extended period, the process can trigger short-term trending that adversely impacts the prices a trader obtains. And there is one more thing: selling (or buying) conveys a negative (or positive) signal for a stock that causes price movements that other participants will jump on, thereby creating a price trend that augments the market impact cost for a large order.

Along with reducing returns, trading costs also cause investors to rebalance their portfolios less frequently. Accordingly, this results in investors holding portfolios that, in a costless environment, they would not deem optimal.

Some trading desks employ a metric called *implementation shortfall* (IS) to measure trading costs. IS is the difference between the price of an actual trade (after taking into consideration all commissions, fees, and taxes) and the price of a hypothetical trade based on a benchmark value. A commonly used benchmark is the midpoint of the national best bid and offer (NBBO), either at the time the trade decision was made or when the process of getting the order executed was first initiated. IS can be seen as a proxy of how good a trader is at implementing his/her trading decisions.

[3] Short selling is defined as selling shares you do not own but have borrowed. You borrow them from your broker with the hope of buying them back later at a lower price to close out your short position.

2.3 What Drives Trading?

In this section, we address a fundamental question: what drives trading? The various players in the market include speculators, hedgers, arbitrageurs, and market makers. On any given trading day, players who are meeting in the marketplace have different investment goals, different time horizons, and different appetites for risk and liquidity. The players also have different amounts of information and different (divergent) expectations about the stock. As this diverse set of players meet, the mixture leads to trading. As noted in the previous section (and we will repeat here), divergent expectations are attributable to information sets being huge, complex, imprecise, incomplete, inaccurate, and ambiguous.

Not only do participants have different expectations, they can also change their individual valuations at any time, either because of their own independent reassessments or upon learning the thoughts of others. A divergence of expectations, along with the attending interdependencies between different people's valuations, profoundly affects the dynamic process of price formation.

Trading results from two different types of shocks: *information shocks* and *liquidity shocks*. Information shocks are due to the advent of news concerning a company, its industry, and/or the macroeconomy.[4] For instance, at the microeconomic (firm/industry) level, a drug company receives FDA approval for a new drug, and its expected 1-year forward share price shoots up. Or at the macroeconomic level, the chairman of the Federal Reserve announces positive unanticipated information about the prospects for the US economy, and major stock indexes vault higher.

All other reasons for trading are referred to as liquidity shocks. The meaning of "liquidity" when used with respect to a "liquidity shock" differs from "liquidity" when used with respect to the "liquidity of a market." We turn to the liquidity of a market later in the chapter.

Regarding liquidity shocks, they occur, not because of the advent of new information, but because of a change in some investors' individual desires to hold shares of a stock. For instance, an individual comes into money and buys shares, or needs money and sells shares. Or he/she has reassessed his/her expectation of a stock's 1-year forward price, or his/her risk and/or illiquidity tolerances have changed. Liquidity shocks can also be attributed to technical trading and the use of participant-unique algorithmic trading strategies. In contrast to information shocks that investors generally respond to in similar (but not necessarily identical) fashion, liquidity shocks are independent (uncorrelated) from investor to investor. Following a liquidity shock that pushes a stock's price away from an equilibrium value, the price will revert back toward the equilibrium it was pushed away from. On the other hand, an information shock changes a stock's equilibrium value, and there will be no reversion back.

[4] In Chap. 3 on macroeconomics, we offer a detailed exploration of how information shocks can affect trading and the liquidity of financial markets.

2.4 Price Discovery: A Major Function of a Marketplace

Price discovery means finding a stock's value that best reflects the broad market's desire to hold its shares. For a simple reason, the process is protracted and complex: investors have divergent expectations. Let us consider a highly simplified example. Assume that some investors value a stock at $25 a share while others value it at $24. What then should the stock's price be? This can be determined only by participants submitting their orders to the market and by their orders being translated into trades and transaction prices.

Good price discovery is, of course, important for those individuals who are participating in a trade.[5] It is also important for a broad array of other uses: derivatives trading, estate valuations, mutual fund valuations and redemptions, marking positions to market, and dark pool pricing.[6] Market-produced prices are also important to firms for assessing their costs of capital, for making share and stock options/warrants issuance and repurchase decisions, and for computing various price-related ratios (for instance, price-to-earnings and market-to-book ratios).

Price discovery, however, is not the only challenge. Quantity discovery is another big one. Institutional participants, because they want to minimize the market impact of their large orders, approach the market wrapped in a veil of secrecy. How do they find each other and trade if they are all trying to stay hidden? Answer: not easily and not always successfully. Large traders commonly "hold their orders in their pockets" or send them to an off-exchange, non-transparent trading facility (commonly referred to as a dark pool). Large traders also "slice and dice" their orders for submission to a "lit" (public) market, entering them in small pieces over an extended period of time.

2.5 Trading: The Implementation of an Investment Decision

We turn next to differentiating trading from investing. Before doing so, we call your attention to two important distinctions.

- *Brokers versus dealers*: A broker is an intermediary who, as an agent, brings an investor's orders to the market and, for this service, is paid a commission. A dealer (also called a market maker) trades with the investor, not as an agent, but as a principal who buys shares from customers who want to sell and who sells shares to customers who want to buy. In further contrast to a broker, the dealer does not charge a commission but instead posts bid quotes

[5] We discuss price discovery due to information arrival in Chap. 3.

[6] Marking to market is an accounting practice that involves restating the value of an asset to reflect its current market levels. A dark pool is a private financial forum for trading securities. We discuss dark pools in Sect. 2.8.

at which he/she will buy that are lower than the ask quotes at which he/she will sell.

- *Sell-side traders versus buy-side traders*: Investment banks and brokerage houses, either as brokers or dealers, are on the sell side of the market, selling trading services to buy-side customers. On the buy side of the market are retail customers and institutional investors. In the past, order handling and trading were predominantly done by the sell side but, in the advanced markets of today, many large institutional investors have their own well-developed trading desks.

With an eye on institutional investors, let us consider the difference between portfolio managers and buy-side traders. Investment decisions are made by portfolio managers while, as part of the same company, a separate entity referred to as a *buy-side trading desk* handles the implementation of the investment decisions. On both the buy side and the sell side, much experience is needed to be a good trader. On the buy side, a good trading desk can add to the overall performance of a portfolio. The opposite is also true – a poor trading desk can impair overall fund performance.

Trading, like investing, is a "professionalized" activity, but traders have a different career path than portfolio managers, and their skill sets are different. Like portfolio managers, traders require solid educational training, and continuing education is also called for in the ever-changing, complex world in which they operate. Traders need to keep up to date with technology, market structure innovations, and, of course, regulatory requirements.

Time has a different meaning for traders than for portfolio managers. A portfolio manager can take days, weeks, and, at times, a good deal longer to investigate a stock's risk, return, and liquidity characteristics. But once an investment decision has been made and is passed to the trading desk, the clock accelerates and time acquires a different meaning. For a trader who has been given an order to work at the start of a trading day, 12:00 noon can seem like the long run. So we ask: what occurs in the short run that makes time so important? The answer: accentuated intraday price volatility.

2.6 Intraday Price Volatility

The challenge and excitement that attend trading are attributable to one thing: the turbulent price movements that occur over brief intervals of time (even within subseconds). In an environment of accentuated intraday volatility, market prices will move sharply in very brief intervals of time, and as they do, trading opportunities suddenly pop up and then quickly vanish. A trading desk's own order handling decisions can cause adverse price moves, and poor order placement and imperfect market timing are costly. When costs are incurred, the gains that an asset manager might otherwise have realized from a good investment decision can be seriously eroded.

When focusing on volatility, think not of prices themselves but of percentage price changes that we refer to as "returns." While we commonly say "price

Exhibit 2.1 Variance ratios

	Open/Day	Close/Day	Day/Month
ALL S&P500	4.36	1.82	1.31
TOP 50 SIZE	3.50	1.40	1.35

volatility," we actually measure the standard deviation or variance of returns. Short-run (for instance, daily) stock return variances are substantially greater than long-run (for instance, monthly) stock return variances. However, there would not have been a difference between short-term and long-term varience if the intraday prices were efficiently set. The accentuation can be seen with reference to Exhibit 2.1.

Exhibit 2.1 shows ratios for opening half-hour to daily, closing half-hour to daily, and daily to monthly variances for SP 500 stocks during 2019.[7] We calculate these ratios for each stock separately and present the average ratio. We adjust for measurement interval length by multiplying the numerator by 13 (the number of half-hour periods per day) for the open/day and the close/day ratios and by 21 (the number of trading days per month) for the day/month ratios. In row 1, we present the average ratio for all SP 500 stocks, and in row 2, we present the average for the top 50 stocks in terms of market capitalization. The accentuation of shorter period volatility is evident from the ratios shown: all are considerably greater than one, where one is the value that represents the benchmark for a perfect, frictionless market. The ratio is especially high for the open/day measure, as the opening half-hour is a period of price discovery (and hence accentuated volatility) following the overnight market close. Later in this chapter, we consider various marketplace realities that can account for the accentuated turbulence of intraday prices. At this point, we turn to a key finance variable: liquidity.

2.7 Liquidity

Liquidity is of major importance for equity markets. However, as we have previously said, it is not subject to simple definition and quantification, and for large investors in particular, finding it is a never-ending challenge. Liquidity is usually thought of in terms of both transaction time (the time it takes to complete a trade) and transaction cost (including the bid-ask spread and market impact). But without a good workable definition, an assessment of liquidity is generally based more on people's perceptions than on generally accepted quantitative analysis. One thing, however, is quite apparent: when a market lacks liquidity, participants know it. For small cap stocks in particular, the illiquidity problem is especially acute, and as such, it has attracted intensified regulatory attention.

Across the broad spectrum of companies and for the economic growth of the entire macroeconomy, liquid, well-functioning markets are of major importance. A stock market, by offering liquidity, gives people the ability to easily buy and sell

[7] We included only the stocks that remained in the index the whole year.

shares when desired. With regard to selling, the need for an exit door is particularly critical. Investors will not buy a stock in the first place if they have insufficient assurance that they will be able to sell it sometime in the future with reasonable facility and at a reasonable price. As we just said, this is particularly important for small companies that are looking to raise money in the primary markets where new shares are issued.

So how might the liquidity of a market be quantitatively assessed? Liquidity has been viewed as the depth, breadth, and resiliency of a market. Depth refers to the size of posted orders that are at or close in price to the best bid and offer in the market. Breadth refers to having orders at numerous price points up and down the order book in relatively close proximity to the best bid and offer. Together, depth and breadth represent the number and size of revealed orders on the book. If the book has sufficient depth and breadth, orders can be executed quickly and in reasonable size.

Resiliency is a stock price's ability to retain an equilibrium value and to speedily regain an equilibrium value if pushed away by a liquidity shock. To repeat, resiliency encompasses two dimensions: (1) the initial impact of a liquidity shock and (2) the speed with which a dislocation is repaired. The initial magnitude depends on the breadth and depth of the market, and the bounce-back depends on the existence of unrevealed, latent liquidity.

Liquidity is supplied in two different ways: revealed (posted) liquidity and latent (not posted) liquidity. Revealed liquidity includes the quotes posted by dealers and by limit orders traders. But some traders' orders are not displayed, and these are the latent ones. Latent orders include orders with special conditions (such as "fill or kill" or "all or nothing" instructions identified in Sect. 2.1). Latent liquidity also includes orders that are "held in traders' pockets" while being worked strategically by a broker. Orders kept on investors' trading desks are also latent (their revelation to a market is commonly triggered by machine-driven algos). Because price moves can trigger the entry of latent liquidity into the market, latent liquidity is dynamic (as opposed to revealed orders on the book which are static). Static (posted) liquidity can be measured, while dynamic (non-revealed) liquidity is not observable. Accordingly, it is not possible to obtain a sufficiently broad measure of this vitally important characteristic of a market. However, illiquidity's *footprint* in a market can be assessed. In Sect. 2.6, we have called attention to illiquidity's big footprint: accentuated intraday price volatility.

2.8 Equity Market Structures

How orders are turned into trades depends on the rules and regulations that define a market's structure. Much development has occurred on the market structure front in recent years with striking technological advances, the emergence of new trading facilities, and an intensification of intermarket competition. Nevertheless, despite some positive developments, two issues have remained challenging: (1) providing

	Bid Size	Bid	Ask	Ask Size	
			24.55	10	
			24.54	50	
			24.53	12	
			24.52	10	
Bid-Ask Spread			24.51	4	
(24.51 – 24.49)	0	24.50			
	5	24.49			
Air pocket	0	24.48			
	100	24.47			
	20	24.46			
	15	24.45			

Exhibit 2.2 Limit order book for ABC stock

reasonable liquidity for smaller stocks and, for all stocks, (2) amassing sufficient liquidity for large, institutional-sized orders.

Trading systems can be classified according to three generic structures:

1. *Continuous order-driven markets.* A market is continuous if a trade can be made whenever, in continuous time, a buy and a sell order meet in price. In an order-driven market, prices are established by posted limit orders. Limit orders to sell set the prices at which market order traders can buy, and limit orders to buy set the prices at which market order traders can sell. The limit orders are posted on a "limit order book," and in continuous trading, a trade is made whenever a buy order matches (or crosses) a sell order during normal trading hours (US markets open at 9:30 am and close at 4:00 pm). A representative limit order book for a continuous order-driven market is shown in Exhibit 2.2.
2. *Periodic call auctions.* In contrast to a continuous order-driven market, a call auction is a periodic order-driven market. With a call auction, participant orders are batched together for simultaneous execution at a single point in time, such as at the opening or closing of the trading day, and all executed orders transact at the same price – the *clearing price*. When the market is called, all buy orders equal to and greater than the clearing price are executable, as are all sell orders equal to or less than the clearing price. Clearing prices are set at values that maximize the number of shares that execute. By batching multiple orders and transactions together, a call auction concentrates liquidity, and in so doing, it can decrease intraday price volatility and reduce transaction costs for participants.[8] A representative limit order book for a call auction is shown in Exhibits 2.3 and 2.4.

[8] The integration of revealed and latent liquidity could be better harmonized in a call auction as the latent liquidity provider could be more comfortable with revealing the orders in a batched trading, periodic environment. Why? For one reason: he/she can get price improvement.

Indicative Price	Bids	Cumulative	Price	Cumulative	Asks	Shares that would Trade
	0	0	24.55	402	97	0
	0	0	24.54	305	42	0
	25	25	24.53	263	55	25
	23	48	24.52	208	69	48
	15	63	24.51	139	32	63
	19	82	24.50	107	27	82
24.49	**26**	**108**	**24.49**	**90**	**38**	**90**
	24	132	24.48	52	32	52
	76	208	24.47	20	20	20
	84	292	24.46	0	0	0
	67	359	24.45	0	0	0

Exhibit 2.3 Call auction book

Indicative Price	Bids	Cumulative	Price	Cumulative	Asks	Shares that would Trade
	0	0	24.55	402	97	0
	0	0	24.54	305	42	0
	25	25	24.53	263	55	25
	23	48	24.52	208	69	48
	45	93	24.51	139	32	93
$24.50	**19**	**112**	**24.50**	**107**	**27**	**107**
	26	138	24.49	90	38	90
	24	162	24.48	52	32	52
	76	238	24.47	20	20	20
	84	322	24.46	0	0	0
	67	389	24.45	0	0	0

Exhibit 2.4 Call auction book following the submission of another buy order (of 30 lots at $24.51)

3. *Continuous dealer markets.* In a dealer market, multiple dealers (also called market makers) post the prices at which public customers can buy or sell shares. A dealer posts two-sided quotes: a bid quote at which the market maker will buy shares from a customer looking to sell and an ask quote at which the market maker will sell shares to a customer looking to buy. A dealer market is commonly referred to as *quote driven* (in contrast with the *order driven* market that we have just discussed). Dealers do not speculate in long-term price movements

Dealer	Bid	Ask	Dealer
Lion	20.40	20.41	Tiger
Fox	20.39	20.42	Bull
Tiger	20.38	20.42	Fox
Bear	20.38	20.43	Lion
Bull	20.37	20.44	Bear

Exhibit 2.5 Dealer market

of the instruments they trade. Instead, they seek to profit from small differences between their buying and selling prices, and they generally hold positions for short periods of time. The adage "stock sold to a dealer is still for sale" captures this reality of a quote-driven environment. A representative screen for a quote-driven market is shown in Exhibit 2.5.

2.8.1 Hybrid Markets

Hybrid markets combine call auctions and continuous trading. Stock exchanges internationally open and close their continuous markets with a call auction. Moreover, when under stress, price discovery can break down in the continuous market, and when this occurs, trading is halted and a call auction is used to reopen the market. The call auction reopening procedure is used because batching orders in multilateral, call auction trading facilitates order handling, sharpens price discovery, and enhances transparency. Call auctions, however, do not provide immediacy, but continuous markets do. Immediacy is appealing to many market participants, and thus, a hybrid market structure that combines these two market structures offers significant advantages.

2.8.2 Handling Large Orders

There are additional procedures available to meet the specialized trading needs of large participants:

1. Block trading is used for the sizable orders of large investors (typically institutional) who are trying to minimize the adverse impacts their large orders have.
2. Large orders can be negotiated by telephone or via an electronic interface.
3. To achieve better executions, a trader will commonly "slice and dice" a large "parent order" into smaller "child orders" that are sequentially submitted to the market over a longer period of time.
4. Also on the scene are "dark pools," trading facilities that allow orders to be entered without disclosing participants' trading interests.

Dark pools, so named to emphasize their lack of transparency, are private trading forums as opposed to public exchanges like the New York Stock Exchange and Nasdaq that are referred to as "lit" because of their higher levels of transparency. While dark pools came about primarily to facilitate block trading by institutional investors, they are also being used for trading small, internalized retail-sized orders received by brokerage houses.[9] That is, the orders are being executed without having been sent to a public exchange.

So here is the situation:

1. Price discovery takes place through trading in public exchanges.
2. These prices are used for trading in the dark pools.
3. Much quantity discovery takes place in the dark pools, particularly for large investors.

The partial separation of price discovery and quantity discovery is not without drawbacks. Equilibrium values for price and quantity are better attained when the price and quantity variables are solved for simultaneously.

2.9 Financial Markets and the Process of Turning Orders into Trades

In this section, we drill down in more detail on how orders are handled and turned into trades in continuous order-driven markets, in call auctions, and in dealer (quote-driven) markets, the three primary market structures.

2.9.1 Trades in Continuous Order-Driven Markets

As we discussed earlier, in the continuous order-driven market, prices are determined by limit orders that are placed in what is referred to as a "limit order book." How does this work? Let us take a closer look.

As we have noted, a market order does not specify a price, whereas a limit order does. A limit price is a maximum price for buy orders and a minimum price for sell orders (which is why they are referred to as "limit orders"). In continuous trading, limit orders generally execute at the price at which they have been entered, while limit orders in a call auction, unless their price is the same as the clearing price, are price improved.

We have said this before, but it merits repeating. Traders who place limit orders avoid paying the bid-ask spread. Those who place market orders incur the cost represented by the spread. But limit order placers incur the risk that their orders might never execute. Also, if a limit order does execute, it could be at a disadvantageous

[9] Internalization occurs when a brokerage firm that has received both buy and sell orders matches and executes them internally rather than sending them to an exchange.

price (buying at a share price as it starts to fall because of the arrival of unanticipated negative news, or selling at a share price as it starts to rise because of the arrival of unanticipated positive news). Because limit order traders face these risks, they require an incentive for being a liquidity provider, and saving the spread is their compensation.

Exhibit 2.2 shows how a limit order book might look for a hypothetical stock, ABC. The exhibit shows limit orders to buy ("bids") at prices ranging from $24.45 to $24.49 and limit orders to sell ("asks," which are also referred to as "offers") at prices ranging from $24.51 to $24.55. The columns labeled "bid size" and "ask size" show the number of round lots entered at each limit order price (a round lot is 100 shares). For example, in the bid size column, the number "5" at $24.49 indicates that there are five "round lots" (500 shares) to buy ABC stock at a price of $24.49. These 500 shares might be one trader's order or multiple traders' orders because the limit order book aggregates all orders that are entered at a given price.

Exhibit 2.2 displays two prices where there are no orders on the book ($24.50 and $24.48). The zero bid size at 24.48 is a gap in the order book that can occur when the market for ABC stock is not very liquid. Gaps such as this one are *air pockets*, and they are present when an order book is "thin" (not "deep"). Ideally, we would like the order book to be deep and to have no air pockets.

The absence of orders at $24.50 is not an air pocket. It is a price point within the bid-ask spread. As we have noted, the spread is the lowest ("best") offer ($24.51) minus the highest ("best") bid ($24.49). In Exhibit 2.2, the spread is shown to be $0.02 per share (two cents). The two-cent spread can exist when the minimum price change is one cent because, for a strategic reason, no participant has chosen to post a limit order within one cent of a counterpart order. To understand this strategic reason, consider a buyer who is entertaining the possibility of placing a limit order at $24.50 when, for one cent more, he/she could buy with certainty at $24.51. With a one cent spread, there is not much to save by placing a limit order and more to lose because of the chance that it will not execute. Thus, the certainty of executing at $24.51 exerts a "pull" on the incoming order, and the pull keeps it from being entered at $24.50. So instead of placing a limit order at $24.50, the buyer enters a market order that executes at $24.51. The pull of certainty accounts for spreads that are wider than the minimum price change of one penny. It is this "pull of certainty" that explains why the absence of an order within the spread is not just another air pocket.

Exhibit 2.2 shows a snapshot of the order book at a single point in time. In the order book shown in Exhibit 2.2, a market order to buy will execute at the best offer ($24.51), and a market order to sell will execute at the best bid ($24.49). These posted prices will change over time as new orders arrive and as existing orders are executed or cancelled.

Suppose that a new market order to buy 5000 shares (50 round lots) is submitted to ABC's limit order book. As shown in Exhibit 2.2, the number of shares available at the best offer of $24.51 is only four round lots (400 shares). This means that not all of the 5000 shares to buy by market order can be purchased at the best asking price of $24.51. In this case, the order will *walk the book*. Walking the book means that any market order that exceeds the size shown at the best quote will trade at ever higher prices (if it is a buy order) or at ever lower prices (if it is a sell order) until it is filled. Accordingly, with walk-the-book pricing, the first 400 shares of the 5000 share order are bought at $24.51, the next 1000 shares are bought at $24.52, the next 1200 shares are bought at $24.53, and the last 2400 shares are bought at $24.54.

The overall purchase price of $24.5312 for the 5000 shares is a weighted average of the four different execution prices, where the weights are the numbers of shares traded at each price point. We thus have ((4 × 24.51) + (10 × 24.52) + (12 × 24.53) + (24 × 24.54))/50 = $24.5312. Because this buy order is much larger than the number of shares available for sale at the best offering price ($24.51), the overall weighted average price of $24.5312 is 2.12 cents per share higher. For the 5000 share order, the additional cost is $106 ($0.0212 × 5000). The higher purchase price will, of course, reduce the buyer's net return on ABC's stock. These additional costs add up and compound over time because they can be incurred each time the investor trades.

2.9.2 Trades in Call Auction Markets

As discussed earlier, a call auction is a periodic (as opposed to a continuous) order-driven market. With a call auction, participants' orders are batched together for simultaneous execution at a single clearing price at a pre-announced point in time. When the market is called, all buy orders equal to and greater than the clearing price are executable, as are all sell orders equal to or less than the clearing price. Trading prices are set at values that maximize the number of shares that execute.

By batching many transactions together, a call auction concentrates liquidity. In so doing, it can significantly decrease transaction costs for participants. Calls also facilitate better "quantity discovery" because they allow larger orders to be executed with reduced information leakage and thus lower market impact costs.[10] Large buyers and sellers who might be reluctant to send their orders to a continuous market may submit them to the call because of market impact costs being lower. The integration of revealed and latent liquidity could also be better achieved in a call auction because latent liquidity providers can get price improvement (with rare exceptions, this does not happen with continuous order-driven trading). Two important operational details of any call auction are the pricing mechanism used and how buy-sell imbalances at the call auction price are handled. The usual pricing mechanism in a call auction is to choose the price that maximizes the number of shares that trade. The usual rationing mechanism to deal with an order imbalance is time priority (first in, first out).

Exhibit 2.3 shows the accumulated orders on the book of a call auction. Buy orders accumulate from the high price to lower prices on the left. Sell orders accumulate from the low price to higher prices on the right.

[10]The concern for large buyers / sellers that other traders might find out about their orders which would lead to trades at unfavorable prices is referred to as "information leakage".

For instance, there is a bid to buy 15 round lots priced at $24.51. Anyone who places a bid at $24.51 is surely willing to buy at that price or at a price that is lower. The cumulative quantity to buy at $24.51 is 63 (the number of round lots entered at bid prices of $24.51 and higher). Likewise, the call auction sellers who place an ask at 24.51 per share would certainly be willing to sell at 24.51 and higher. Since there are cumulative numbers of 63 bids and 139 asks at $24.51, the minimum of those numbers, 63 round lots, would trade at that price. The indicative clearing price is the price at which, as we have noted, the maximum number of shares would be traded. In this example, the indicative price is $24.49 with 90 round lots executed (the minimum of 108 cumulative buys and 90 cumulative sells).

Continuing to refer to Exhibit 2.3, you can see that at $24.49, the number of round lots that trade is maximized at 90 by noting that at one tick up, 82 round lots (less than 90) would trade (the minimum of 82 and 107) and that at one tick down, 52 round lots (again less than 90) would trade (the minimum of 52 and 132). Thus, if the market gets called at this instant, $24.49 would be the realized clearing price. The cumulative number of round lots to buy is 108 at $24.49; the 90 out of the 108 that execute is determined by applying the price priority rule. Notice that with an execution price of 24.49, the bids above 24.49 and the asks below 24.49 receive price improvement (i.e., the realized transaction prices are improved vis-à-vis the limit prices on the orders that the participants had submitted to the call).

Now let a new buy order comes in at $24.51 for 30 round lots before the market is called. This will increase the total number of bids by 30 at 24.51 and every price point below it. As a result, the new maximum number of shares that would be traded is now 107 at a new indicative price of $24.50. And so call auctions progress as orders arrive and the book builds. As new orders keep coming in, the indicative price keeps fluctuating until the market is "called," at which point the auction price and the number of shares that trade are established.

We have presented a basic example of call auction trading, but the calls can differ in any number of ways from market to market. For instance, each market would have further rules about how to prioritize the trades when there is an imbalance between the bids and the asks at the clearing price because only by rare chance will the two sides of the market match exactly. When the number of shares on the two sides differs, the lesser of the two sides determines the total number of shares that executes, and shares on the bigger side of the market have to be rationed. Generally, as we have noted, the shares on the larger side that execute are determined by applying a time priority rule (the first orders placed get executed first). If application of the time priority rule does not produce an exact match, a further rationing rule is required, and various alternatives are possible. This is part of the complexity of designing a real-world market. In the example above, these additional rules would govern which 107 bids out of the 112 would end up being executed. Another way in which calls can differ from one another is in the amount of information about the call book that is disseminated while the book is still building prior to when the market is called. The full book may not be revealed, and only the indicated clearing price is shown to the public.

2.9.3 Trades in Continuous Dealer Markets

As described earlier, in a dealer market, dealers state the prices at which public customers can buy or sell shares. Thus, a dealer market is commonly referred to as quote driven. A dealer posts two-sided quotes: a bid quote at which the market maker will buy shares if a customer is looking to sell and an ask quote at which the market maker will sell shares if a customer is looking to buy.

In Exhibit 2.5, we see a market consisting of five competing dealers. In this market. the current best bid is quoted by Lion ($20.40), and the current best ask is quoted by Tiger ($20.41). In other words, Lion is eager to buy, and Tiger is eager to sell, and therefore, they are offering the most aggressive quotes in the market. Their quotes set the NBBO, the national best bid and offer.

Customers may choose to send their orders to any dealer that they prefer regardless of the prices that the dealer is currently quoting. This practice is called *preferencing*. The receiving dealers have the right to reject the orders, but they rarely do. Instead they will accept the order and execute it at the best bid or offer quoted in the market.

Dealers trade against public customers and other dealers. They adjust their quotes as the day progresses, as market conditions evolve, and as their own inventory levels fluctuate. As dealers see substantial portions of the aggregate order flow, they gain insight into the balance between public buying and selling pressures. Collectively, the competing dealers play the central role in discovering prices in the quote-driven environment.

2.10 Regulation, Technology, and the Quality of Market Structure[11]

For many years, three powerful forces have been reshaping the operations and quality of the equity markets: regulation, competition, and technology. In this section, we focus primarily on the first, regulation, and on its interrelation with the other two. In so doing, we concentrate on US markets, but the picture in many ways is the same in other major equity markets around the world. Chapter 4 deals, in further detail, with technology.

Regulators have focused a great deal on competition, primarily on how it exists between the exchanges and other trading venues. In so doing, they have relied, in good part, on competition to drive exchange fees down to competitive levels and to encourage technological innovation. The approach has been effective regarding fees, but it has come at a cost. Strengthening competition between different trading facilities fragments the order flow, and fragmentation can have harmful effects on the quality of price discovery.

[11] This section is a modified reprint with permission of "Perspectives: The Interplay Between Regulation, Competition, and Technology and the Transformation of Our Equity Markets" by Ozenbas and Schwartz, *The Journal of Portfolio Management*, November 2020.

In one way, regulation can impede, not spur, competition and market structure development. New innovations must receive regulatory approval, and because regulators like to proceed with great caution, getting approval is generally a lengthy process. A good example involves the pioneering introduction of the first electronic call auction trading facility, the *Wunsch Auction System*. Founded in 1990, this new market became the Arizona Stock Exchange (AZX) in 1991. Not surprisingly, the New York Stock Exchange (NYSE) did not welcome a novel competitor, and the Securities and Exchange Commission (SEC) was concerned about the effect an electronic call could have on the Big Board's operations.[12] After a great deal of lengthy deliberation, the SEC did give the Wunsch Auction System a green light, but in so doing, the commission imposed a critical restriction: the call auction could not be held until 30 minutes after the market's 4:00 pm close. Not many traders hang around their desks after the main market has closed, and with this constraint, the new trading facility could not succeed. After years of trying, in October 2001, the AZX closed down because of insufficient order flow. But it had been on the right track. In 2020, the dollar volume of trading at the opening and closing calls which were by then being run by the NYSE accounted for about 9.7% of the total daily trading volume of the same stocks.[13]

Technology development has massively transformed the equity markets in the decades that followed the 1975 Amendments. Consider the speed with which orders are handled and turned into trades: in the pre-electronic era, the trade clock ticked at a slow enough pace for humans to follow price formation on a trade-to-trade basis; today, markets can change from microsecond to microsecond, and the trade-to-trade evolution of price formation cannot be followed by eye, only by computer. Consider the fragmentation of the order flow: in the past, the New York Stock Exchange enjoyed an 80% market share for its listed stocks; today, the NYSE's market share is hovering around 20%, and trading is dispersed over roughly 40 dark pool trading facilities and 16 exchanges. Consider the intermarket linkages: they used to be weak and slow; today's electronic markets are fast and interconnected, not only across exchanges and the off-exchange facilities but also between the stock and derivative markets. Consider how trades are accomplished: in the past, they were made by human-to-human interaction, either face-to-face or by phone; in today's super rapid, super interconnected markets, trades are also being made by computer orders meeting computer orders without direct human intervention (i.e., computer-driven algorithmic – algo – trading).

There is another big one we can thank technology for: the availability of data. In 1975, end of day, closing prices were reported in the papers, and that was about it; today, we have electronically delivered, intraday data with a microsecond time stamp for quotes, prices, trading volumes, and market indices, and the sheer amount of this data is enormous. Additionally, detailed audit trails are now available for regulators to peruse.

[12] "Big Board" is a common nickname for the NYSE.

[13] Calculated by the authors using 2020 data from the TAQ and CRSP databases for 2593 stocks listed on the NYSE (some small stocks were eliminated due to missing data).

Put this together and what do we have? We have speed, we have competition, we have an extraordinarily complex environment, and the regulators are faced with a huge challenge with regard to their obligation to police the markets for abuses of power and position.[14] Moreover, the electronic markets can be fragile. With electronic order submission and executions, every condition must be planned for because preprogramed computers cannot implement adjustments that human participants are capable of making when they are given reasonable freedom to do so. That is, a computer code has to be rewritten, while a human can make adjustments and corrections on the fly. Does this reality call for further regulatory intervention, or should the markets be left to sort it out by themselves?

Two things are clear: (1) the markets are the innovators, and (2) keeping regulations properly aligned with ever-evolving market structures is necessary but not easily accomplished. Regulatory oversight is necessary because of the enormous importance equity markets have for the macroeconomy, because a technological breakdown can have disastrous impacts on the financial markets, and because a poorly functioning secondary market (where already listed shares are traded) can make it more difficult for listed companies to raise funds in the primary markets (where new shares are issued). However, good regulatory policy is extraordinarily difficult to formulate. The issues are complex and regulatory intervention can give rise to *unintended consequences* (in medicine, "unintended consequences" are called "side effects"). In part, the complexity is attributable to various issues being very thorny. Here are three examples:

- There is a trade-off between promoting intermarket competition (which calls for fragmenting the order flow across trading venues) and promoting competition within the order flow (which calls for consolidating the order flow). What is the right balance between these two kinds of competition?
- All participants value transparency (the rapid public display of transaction prices, quotes, and trading volume). However, many participants, large institutional investors in particular, do not want their own trading intensions disclosed. So how should the conflict between the collective desire for transparency and the individual needs for opacity be resolved?
- Free competition between firms has been widely relied on in the United States to advance economic development, and for much of its history, market structure has evolved naturally in a free environment. Government (with exceptions of course) does not tell a firm such as GAP how exactly to produce clothes. Should it be

[14] Manipulating a market by "spoofing," for instance, presents a particularly interesting challenge to regulators. Spoofing is the act of placing a bid or offer quote with the *intent* of cancelling the quote before it executes. Note the word "intent." How might regulators infer a trader's intent from his or her order placement decisions? There can be valid reasons for withdrawing an order soon after it has been placed. To name two: (1) the broad market or the market for the specific stock has changed, and (2) the trader has placed orders for two or more stocks and one or more of them has executed. Also, detecting and controlling spoofing is far from a simple matter because orders can be submitted to a sizable number of alternative facilities as well as to the futures and options markets. So this is what the regulators face: intent is hard to prove, and in the complexity of the markets, manipulators can find cover.

telling the equity markets how to produce trades and transaction prices? Yes, some government intervention in equity market structure development is no doubt called for, but what should the balance be between free market development and regulatory intervention?

Government regulation in the US equity markets operates on three levels: the US Congress, the Securities and Exchange Commission (SEC, established in 1934), and on the state level. In addition, equity markets have their own *self-regulatory organizations* (SROs). The New York Stock Exchange and the National Association of Securities Dealers had their own SROs until July 2007 when the SEC approved the merger of the two to form the Financial Industry Regulatory Authority (FINRA).

For the most part, regulation exists to police the markets for abuses of power and position, including fraud, manipulation, and trading on insider information. However, for almost half a century, government regulation by the Congress and the SEC has extended into overseeing the very structure of the securities markets.

The first major government regulatory foray into market structure occurred when the US Congress enacted the 1975 Amendments to the Securities Exchange Act of 1934. At the time, the Congress was concerned about the extent to which equity market dealers were profiting from unduly wide bid-ask spreads, and they were unhappy that commissions had been fixed at unjustifiably high levels. In addition, the amendments were enacted following the creation of the Securities Investor Protection Corporation (SIPC) in 1970 by an act of the Congress. SIPC is a nonprofit corporation that financially protects the clients of its member brokerage firms if those brokerage firms are forced into bankruptcy. Consequently, government, having become directly involved in the financial stability of the broker-dealers, now had a vested interest in these firms staying healthy and avoiding bankruptcy.

The Amendments included two items of particular importance: (1) it precluded trading commissions from ever being fixed (as they previously had been), and (2) it mandated the development of a *National Market System (NMS)*. Regarding the NMS, four objectives were stipulated:

- Enhance the economic efficiency of transactions (i.e., reasonable transaction costs).
- Ensure fair competition among brokers, dealers, and markets.
- Ensure the broad availability of information on quotations and transactions.
- Provide the opportunity, consistent with efficiency and best execution, for investors' orders to be executed without the participation of a dealer.

The SEC was charged with implementing the 1975 Amendments. This was not an easy task. For starters, in mandating the development of a National Market System, the Congress provided no definition of what an NMS was. Much discussion, many meetings, and a number of conferences followed, and further regulations were enacted.

Today, the markets are far more connected by computers, various trading costs have been reduced, and considerably more information on quotes and transactions is available (thanks again to computers). And with regard to the fourth bullet above, dealers are far less prominent in today's equity markets. However, further regulations were enacted with respect to achieving the goals of the 1975 legislation. Below are four regulatory developments in particular that affected the role played by competition, that were initiated by the SEC over the years that followed the Securities Acts Amendments of 1975.

1997: Order Handling Rules. Comprehensive changes were mandated in 1997 by the SEC in the rules governing share trading in the United States. Known as *Order Handling Rules*, the regulation effectively ended market makers' dominance in price setting. These rules primarily affected Nasdaq, the world's second-largest stock market at the time (following the New York Stock Exchange), as Nasdaq was primarily designed as a dealer market. More transparency was required. Moreover, the previously private electronic systems used to trade big orders were opened up to the public. As a result, prices on these systems, which were often better than those offered by the market makers, became visible and available to the public. Following this regulatory initiative, several new execution venues including alternative trading systems (ATSs) and electronic communication networks (ECNs) opened.[15] Their arrival led the way to a steady decrease in the market share of all traditional stock markets (including Nasdaq and the NYSE).

2001: Decimalization. The SEC ordered all US stock markets to convert to trading in decimals by April 2001. Prior to this date, prices had been quoted in 1/8ths and, more recently, in 1/16ths of a dollar, as opposed to decimals, the norm in other international equity markets.[16] The main intent of this rule was to decrease the bid-ask spread and, hence, one of the costs of trading. With decimal pricing, the minimum tick size shrunk to a penny and bid-ask spreads thightened. This, however, had another consequence: decreased spreads made dealer operations significantly less profitable and the structure of the dealer market changed.

NYSE Rule 390. On May 17, 1792, twenty four stockbrokers signed an agreement at 68 Wall Street in New York City. According to legend, they met under a buttonwood tree, and the document they signed became known as the Buttonwood Agreement. It was historic. The Buttonwood Agreement marked the founding of the New York Stock Exchange.

---

[15] Electronic communication networks (ECNs) are a type of alternative trading system (ATS) that trades listed stocks and other exchange-traded products. Unlike dark pools, another type of ATS, ECNs, display orders in the consolidated quote stream. Like ATSs, ECNs are required to register with the commission as broker-dealers and are also members of FINRA.

[16] The 1/8th quotation dated from the colonial period, when the most common unit of currency used was the Spanish dollar, also known as "piece of eight," where a Spanish dollar was worth 8 Spanish silver reales.

The 24 brokers agreed on two points: their commissions were fixed at 0.25%, and they were to deal only with each other. Eventually, their agreement to deal only with each other became codified as NYSE Rule 390. Specifically, Rule 390 stated that an exchange member receiving an order for an exchange listed stock must bring that order to an exchange floor to be executed, that off-floor trading by exchange members was prohibited.

With regard to off-floor trading, in carrying out its congressional mandate, the SEC announced in June 1977 that NYSE Rule 390 was to be removed by the end of the year. A loud outcry against this was successfully raised by the industry, and at the last minute, the SEC postponed the rule's removal. But the threat of removal remained.

What motivated the regulators to seek Rule 390's elimination? In 1975, the NYSE was far and away the dominant exchange. Central to the exchange's market model was the specialist, a market maker who had the affirmative obligation to make a fair and orderly market for the stocks traded at his or her post. The NYSE's market share of the order flow was enormous, and all the orders for a specific stock went to the trading post of the specific specialist firm to which the stock was assigned. So think about it. Where in this model was competition? Where were the substantial competitive pressures that would keep trading fees low and innovation robust? These are the questions the regulators asked, and they did not like the answers.

However, in one way, the NYSE did face competition. Historically, there has been intense competition between the three largest exchanges in the United States – the NYSE, Nasdaq, and the American Stock Exchange (AMEX). Each has fought hard to attract the new listings of corporations that are going public and to get companies that are already public to switch their listings. This competition has certainly given the exchanges an incentive to improve the quality of their markets. But is this form of competition sufficient?

In any event, the battle over Rule 390 continued. The next regulatory action was in 1980 when a new SEC rule, Rule 19c-3, became effective. The new rule chipped away at Rule 390 by permitting the off-board trading of stocks that were listed after April 26, 1979. However, the 19c-3 stocks were relatively few in number, the large proportion of NYSE stocks remained subject to 390, and 19c-3 did not deliver the results the SEC was looking for. But the commission did not give up. Finally, on May 8, 2000, NYSE Rule 390 was repealed.

What effect did the repeal have? In the years and months leading up to May 2000, the NYSE's market share hovered around 80% to 90%. It took some time for participants to adapt and for the order flow to respond, but then the exchange's market share dropped precipitously. In 2003, it had fallen to 50%, and by 2019, it was hovering around 20%. What the regulators were looking for they got. The markets did become a great deal more competitive.

Regulation National Market System (Reg NMS) and the Order Protection Rule. Reg NMS is a set of rules established by the SEC in 2007 that are designed to further strengthen the competitive structure of the US equity market. The major provision in Reg NMS that we focus on here is the Order Protection Rule. To ensure that investors buy and sell at the best available prices, the Order Protection Rule requires that the most aggressive quotes (highest bids and lowest offers) across the different trading venues be protected. Alternatively stated, the rule disallows executing a trade at a price inferior to the best bid and offer quotes (the protected quotes) in the market. For instance, if the best bid on Venue A is \$20.12 and the best bid on Venue B is \$20.15, an incoming sell order must be sent to and executed against B's quote of \$20.15. If the seller's order were to execute against A's \$20.12 quote, B's higher bid would have been "traded through." For this reason, the Order Protection Rule is also referred to as the Trade Through Rule.

The Order Protection Rule can certainly come across as being fair and reasonable. Think of how the buyer who entered the higher bid in Venue B would feel if his or her \$20.15 posting was traded through by a trade made in Venue A at the lower price of \$20.12. But do not forget that each quote has not only a price but also a size component to it. What if the incoming sell order is for 10,000 shares while, concurrently, the \$20.15 bid in Venue B is for 200 shares and the \$20.12 bid in Venue A is for 12,000 shares? And what if realizing a fast execution is of critical importance for the seller? Let us ask the question this way: should investors seeking large volume trades be required to first access small-sized quotations? Should venues be denied the ability to compete by offering good trading possibilities at prices above or below the national best bid and offer (NBBO)? What is a fair, equitable, and efficient way to direct order flow to different venues in a fragmented market? And speaking of fragmentation, a result of Reg NMS was more trading venues opening up, which further dispersed the order flow. Clearly, with regard to this complex issue, it is easier to ask questions than to provide simple answers to them.

Reg NMS had another effect, one that is attributable to an exception within the bill. Returning to our example, for Venue B's \$20.15 quote to be protected, it had to be immediately and automatically accessible. This exception had a consequence of major importance. The New York Stock Exchange, which for many years had resisted introducing electronic trading, now had no other choice. For its own quotes to be protected, the exchange had to offer fast and automatically accessible quotes. In other words, it had to institute an electronic trading platform. And it did.

The regulations we have discussed were intended to increase competition. They have and, along with technology development, they have had a powerful impact on market structure. Today, the speed with which traders can check quotes in multiple markets has become of major importance. This in turn has given rise to an enormous technology investment and to high frequency trading. Today, there are exchanges. Additionally, private trading platforms are competing with public markets, offering cheaper but, as we discuss earlier in this chapter, largely nontransparent alternatives to public exchanges.[17] Put it all together and what do we have? The landscape today is far more complicated.[18] And there is another development of major importance. Today, dealers play a strikingly diminished role in bringing liquidity and price discovery to the markets.

The combined impact of regulation, competition, and technology has indeed transformed equity markets in the United States, and similar developments have been experienced in other major markets around the world. The difference between what markets are today and what they were when the 1975 Securities Acts Amendments were enacted is breathtaking. Few people would want to go back to where we were in the days of old. Nevertheless, problems concerning market quality persist. Intraday volatility remains significantly accentuated. The difficulty of executing large institutional orders remains formidable. Price discovery is still a challenge. The market for small capitalization stocks needs to be improved. And one problem that underlies all of the above persists: markets remain too illiquid, even for the largest capitalization stocks. Accordingly, we end this section with two questions. (1) How can more liquidity be attracted to the market? 2) How can latent (hidden) liquidity be more effectively integrated with revealed liquidity and, better yet, transformed into revealed liquidity?

2.11 Wrapping It Up: Market Efficiency in a Non-frictionless World

We started this chapter by calling your attention to something of critical importance: the relationship between fundamental information and the prices of equity shares. Understanding and appreciating this relationship requires basic institutional knowledge and, importantly, a solid comprehension of the following concepts:

1. Frictionless versus non-frictionless markets
2. Trading decisions versus investment decisions
3. Risk versus return versus liquidity
4. The drivers of trading: information shocks versus liquidity shocks
5. Explicit trading costs versus implicit trading costs
6. Posted liquidity versus latent liquidity
7. Measuring liquidity directly versus assessing illiquidity's footprints in the transactions tape
8. Short-period (e.g., intraday) price volatility versus longer-period (e.g., one month) price volatility

[17] According to the TABB Group, trading in dark pools comprised approximately 39% of all trading volume as of 2019.

[18] One example of complexity is that to attract more order flow, the competing exchanges now have complicated fee structures that include rebates and discounts which are generally referred to as maker-taker fees. The rebates are being payed to traders who add (make) liquidity, while the fees are being charged to traders who take liquidity from the market.

9. Homogeneous expectations versus divergent expectations
10. Price discovery, a major function of a stock exchange
11. Order types, most importantly, limit orders and market orders
12. The structure of an equity market

Let us circle back to the first entry on the list: frictionless versus non-frictionless markets. Think about it. The eleven other items on the list are important only because markets are not frictionless. With this in mind, let us consider the eleven other items on the list with the knowledge that the market is not frictionless.

In a frictionless environment, trading would be irrelevant. In a frictionless environment, only risk versus return would matter because all markets would be perfectly liquid. Liquidity shocks would not impact share prices. Trading costs, either explicit or implicit, would not exist. There would be no differentiation between posted liquidity and latent liquidity. Liquidity would not have to be measured, and there would be no illiquidity footprints in the transaction record. In a perfectly liquid world, short-period price volatility would not be accentuated and thus, if short-period and long-period volatility are both expressed in terms of the same measurement interval (e.g., per month or per year), the two measures would be identical. Because it would be costless to obtain and instantly evaluate all new information, every participant would be completely and identically informed, and under this condition, expectations could be homogenous. Totally accurate price discovery would be instantaneously achieved, and equity shares in the perfectly liquid, frictionless world would have fundamental values. Order submission would be instantaneous and costless, and differentiated order types would not be needed. And what could there possibly be to say about market structure if markets were perfectly liquid?

What do you think of the frictionless world? It is a difficult environment to imagine literally existing, and of course, it does not exist. To achieve a more complete comprehension of the workings of a real-world financial market, the realities of a non-frictionless market must be comprehended. Yet for some purposes, the simplifying assumption that markets are frictionless enables a rigorous, insightful model to be achieved. This certainly is the case for the Capital Asset Pricing Model (CAPM) that we dealt with in Chapter 1. Similarly, the Black-Scholes option pricing model assumes frictionless markets as well.

Analysis of a frictionless market yields another insight. In a frictionless environment, fundamental information is immediately and perfectly incorporated into share prices, and thus, share prices are instantly set with total efficiency. So what could cause a share price to change? Only new, unanticipated information. Current expectations based on the existing information set are not new information. By "new information," we mean totally new and totally unpredictable.

Now, if informational change cannot be predicted, might one still be able to predict what the next price change will be? The answer is a resounding "no." In statistical terms, in the perfectly efficient environment, stock price changes are, from one change to the next, uncorrelated. "Random walk" is the term used to describe this property of an informationally efficient market. Let us be clear: it is returns (price *changes*) that are uncorrelated, and it is *prices* that take a random walk. Now reverse the logic. Because random walk is a property of a perfectly efficient market, random walk tests have been used to assess the informational efficiency of a market and, in so doing, to test the *efficient market hypothesis (EMH)*.

Have the random walk model and the EMH been validated? From our perspective on trading, the most relevant tests of the EMH are based on very short period, intraday data, and the tests have shown that intraday correlation patterns do indeed exist, thereby rejecting the hypothesis. This is consistent with what we said earlier in this chapter about intraday price volatility being accentuated. Both positive and negative intraday correlation patterns exist in complex combinations. However, the patterns keep shifting, and exploiting them with a profitable trading strategy is far from an easy task. Wise traders should recognize and deal with this reality. The intraday correlations say a lot about trading not being simple, and they underscore the need for having a well-designed market structure, along with good market structure regulation.

Equity markets have evolved tremendously in recent decades, and change is continuing apace. This is attributable to the three big drivers: competition, technology, and regulation, all three of which impact market structure. Regarding market structure, aside from issues concerning the abuse of power and position (such as insider trading and price manipulation) and technology's reliability, the quality of a market is equivalent to the quality of its liquidity provision. Illiquidity is a manifestation of impediments in trading that we have referred to as friction. We do not operate in a frictionless environment and never will. No matter how efficient our trading systems, there are limits to how liquid participants can expect a market to be.

Friction distorts the relationship between realized prices and underlying equilibrium values. Accordingly, prices bounce around equilibrium values, short-term volatility is accentuated, and correlation patterns are introduced in the return data. The bottom line is that, in a non-frictionless market, liquidity is not fully available when investment decisions are being implemented. Thus, substantial implementation costs can appreciably lower investment returns, and to the extent that they put downward pressure on share prices, they increase the cost of capital for listed companies.

A major economic raison d'etre for a secondary market (where already listed shares are traded) is to enable shareholders to liquidate their positions with reasonable facility when so desired. But in stock markets today, liquidity is not consistently available for all stocks (both large and small), for all time periods (both throughout the trading day and inter-day), and for all market conditions (both normal and particularly stressful), and the efficient market hypothesis (EMH) should not be totally accepted. But neither should the EMH be totally rejected. It stands as a warning to anyone who thinks they have found a magic bullet, a "sure fire" formula that would enable trading based on mispricing to be consistently profitable.

We conclude this chapter with two thoughts: (1) markets are efficient enough to be a strict disciplinarian for any unduly rambunctious trader, and (2) trading frictions certainly have their dark side, but there is a bright side as well. Jobs exist because of them, and they make work a good deal more challenging, interesting, and exciting. This certainly is the case for equity trading.

Liquidity and the Impact of Information Shocks: A Macroeconomics Course Application

3

The relationship between the macroeconomy and equity share prices is of critical importance. So if that is true, then how does the economy affect equity prices and vice versa? In many cases, it is news about the macroeconomy and, more precisely, *unexpected* news.[1] The release of "surprises" about the economy is referred to as "information shocks" which can have swift and significant effects on stock prices. Information shocks are fundamentally different than the "liquidity shocks" described earlier in the Finance chapter. In the case of liquidity shocks, we saw how the structure of the financial market itself and the quantity and quality of orders submitted can affect the ability of investors to find the "true" price of a stock through a process referred to as "price discovery." In our case here, information shocks also have a large impact on the price discovery process, but the main driver of these shocks is the advent of unexpected news, not the lack of liquidity within a financial market. In this chapter, we describe some examples of macroeconomic-related shocks and their effects on the US stock market, as well as the inter-relationships between financial markets and the economy.

Given the enormous size and complexity of a nation's economy, information related to the macroeconomy covers a wide array of items. What factors are most important? First and foremost are interest rates that apply to individual firms, specific industries, as well as broader sectors of the economy. In macroeconomics, the relationship primarily focuses on the interactions between interest rates, the private sector (comprised of consumers, investors, and businesses), and government policymakers at the Federal Reserve (via monetary policy) and the US Treasury (via fiscal policy). Because interest rates represent the rental price of money, they serve as the

[1] As discussed in the Finance chapter, financial markets can be "informationally efficient" if they process and incorporate unexpected news quickly and correctly into current stock prices. According to the "efficient market hypothesis" (EMH), if markets properly and rapidly impound new information into stock prices, then the behavior of these prices should resemble a "random walk" and thus lead to unpredictable price movements over time. As noted in the Finance chapter, financial markets are reasonably efficient but not always perfect and thus can present opportunities for alert investors and traders to spot price trends before others uncover them.

D. Ozenbas et al., *Liquidity, Markets and Trading in Action*, Classroom Companion: Business, https://doi.org/10.1007/978-3-030-74817-3_3

main link between the "real world" of the macroeconomy and the "financial world" of equity and bond markets. Both the private sector and the government watch interest rates closely as a signal of the economy's current and future condition in order to make better decisions in allocating scarce resources to their most efficient uses. Through the liquidity provided by financial markets, investors can channel their savings to profitable investments which ultimately leads to stronger economic growth for society. Thus, economists and investors should consider the liquidity of financial markets to better understand how the financial and real worlds interact with each other.

3.1 Economic Conditions, Business Cycles, and the Role of Interest Rates

The key driver of business cycle fluctuations in most countries is business investment, and sudden changes in this investment can lead to economic booms as well as recessions. Business executives are therefore constantly assessing the economic landscape to see what consumers are buying (and in what quantities), as well as tracking consumers' confidence in order to decide how much to invest in the future. As consumer demand rises and falls, businesses react quickly by adjusting the amount of investment in plant, equipment, inventories, research, and new technology. These adjustments can lead to sharp changes in employment and wages which ultimately affect further changes in consumers' spending patterns. The relationship between investment and consumption is circular, and this leads to the cyclical nature of most economies, as booms are followed by recessions which eventually lead to recoveries and then further economic booms.

Interest rates are also greatly affected by business investment because firms typically borrow money from lenders and investors in order to finance future expansion. This increased demand for money places upward pressure on interest rates unless a government's central bank such as the U.S. Federal Reserve (commonly referred to as "the Fed") increases the supply of money.

The interaction between investment and interest rates is complex because the effects can be simultaneous in nature. That is, business investment not only affects interest rates, but the level of these rates, in turn, affects the level of investment. For example, if consumers suddenly buy more goods and services, businesses will invest more and ultimately push interest rates up due to an increased demand for money. However, if interest rates rise too high, then businesses will cut back on investment because the cost of financing the new plant and equipment or inventory can now exceed the profit that businesses could earn on this new investment. Eventually, the reduction in investment due to higher interest rates will lead to a lower demand for money. This will then result in lower rates in the future, thus creating a classic cycle between investment and interest rates.

Changes in business investment are, therefore, watched closely by policymakers such as those at the Federal Reserve. The Fed will try to stimulate and stabilize the economy by adjusting the Federal Funds rate in order to maintain steady growth with low inflation.[2] To adjust this key interest rate upward (or downward), the Fed typically uses open market operations ("OMO") to sell (or buy) U.S. Treasury securities in the government bond markets where the primary trading partners are financial institutions such as commercial banks and securities broker-dealers. When the Fed sells U.S. Treasurys via OMO activity, the goal is to reduce the supply of money and increase the Federal Funds rate (assuming the demand for money remains relatively constant). By selling U.S. Treasurys, the Fed is withdrawing dollars from the economy and reducing the money supply because investors have to give up their cash to acquire these government securities. Economists call this a "contractionary" monetary policy because the goal of raising this key rate is to cause banks and other lenders to increase their loan rates and, in so doing, make it more costly for businesses and consumers to afford additional investment and consumption. This can eventually lead to a contraction of the economy by reducing business investment because higher interest rates can "cool off" an economy that might be on the verge of "overheating" through increased price inflation. In contrast, an "expansionary" monetary policy occurs when the Fed buys U.S. Treasurys to inject more money into the economy in order to lower the Federal Funds rate and stimulate greater investment by businesses and consumers.

3.2 The Federal Reserve and the Link Between the Macroeconomy and Financial Markets

The Fed's OMO actions create a constant "interactive feedback loop" between the macroeconomy and financial markets. As macroeconomic conditions and interest rates change, both the Fed and market participants such as banks, brokers, and asset managers adjust their holdings of not only U.S. Treasury securities but also riskier assets such as corporate bonds and equity shares. Investors in financial markets respond to unexpected news about the economy and interest rates because a stock's or bond's value is determined by the present value of its expected future cash flows. As noted in the Microeconomics chapter, this investor reaction is driven by changes in the risk-free rate that can affect the Capital Market Line according to the Capital Asset Pricing Model (CAPM). In that model, as the risk-free rate goes up, the intercept rises, the slope falls, and tangency with the efficient frontier moves up and to the right, thus raising investors' required returns for the market portfolio. The Capital Market Line concept helps explain how the Fed's actions and policy statements can create information shocks that lead to a large amount of trading activity in all types of securities which, in turn, depend on the liquidity of the financial markets. Through this daily trading of literally trillions of dollars' worth of securities, the financial markets serve an important purpose as the primary mechanism for discovering the proper prices of financial assets. As noted earlier in the Finance and Microeconomics chapters, price discovery is a major function of any well-operating financial market.

[2] The Federal Funds rate is the interest rate commercial banks charge each other for overnight borrowings to meet short-term liquidity needs.

A good example of this interactive feedback loop can be seen in the Fed's October 2018 announcement of their plans to continue raising interest rates and in how this contractionary policy jolted the U.S. stock markets and caused a sharp price decline by the end of December 2018. In response to this negative market reaction, the chairman of the Fed, Jerome Powell, stated in early January 2019 that the Fed's contractionary stance would be put on "pause." The financial markets viewed this as good news because it was feared that continued hikes in the Federal Funds rate could cause the U.S. economy to fall into a recession. The U.S. stock market reacted very positively to this change in monetary policy during the first quarter of 2019. Seeing this, the Fed ultimately decided to cut interest rates three times and led to a 29% increase in the S&P 500 during 2019. More details about this example of interactions between the economy and financial markets are discussed later in this chapter.

3.3 The Impact of Information Shocks on Divergent Expectations and Price Discovery

Changes in Fed policy can affect the liquidity of financial markets not only directly by the Fed's OMO activity but also through the information "signals" contained within these policy changes. For example, an unexpected cut in the Federal Funds rate is an information shock that might signal to investors and business executives that the economy is currently weak but, at the same time, lets everyone know that the Fed is acting to stimulate economic conditions and thus will strengthen the macroeconomy in the future. This can create "divergent expectations" (a concept discussed in the Finance chapter) where some relatively pessimistic market participants will trade based on the short-term economic weakness (e.g., by buying bonds which rise in value, causing interest rates to fall, and also by selling stocks). In contrast, more optimistic market participants will focus on the positive prospects of expected future, longer-term economic strength and choose to invest in riskier assets that will perform well in an expanding economy (e.g., by selling bonds and buying stocks).

In financial markets jargon, the pessimistic traders are typically called "bears," while the optimistic traders are described as "bulls." Trading in financial markets between these two types of investors will then help discover the proper "equilibrium" prices of stocks and bonds. These prices are informative signals. However, it might take not only an entire trading day but also several days (or even weeks) for the bulls and bears to trade with each other until a new equilibrium price is discovered. This protracted price discovery process occurs because economic reports released after the initial information shock can sometimes be conflicting in nature. For example, bullish economic data released one day can be followed by bearish data the next day, thus sowing confusion as to what the true impact of these reports will be on a stock's price.

To illustrate the important role of price discovery, a simplified example can be used based on the stock price of a hypothetical firm, ABC. Prior academic research by Handa, Schwartz, and Tiwari (2003) suggests that we can describe the divergence of investor expectations by dividing a set of participants into two groups. Let us call one group the bulls and the other the bears. We can assume the bulls value ABC shares at \$30 and the bears value ABC shares at \$20. The bulls are the buyers, and the bears are the sellers due to their divergence in expectations about the future value of the stock based on some unexpected macroeconomic news such as a sudden change in the Federal Reserve's monetary policy. Let participants arrive sequentially in the financial market and either (1) post orders to buy or to sell or (2) trade immediately at bid or offer prices set by orders that have previously been placed.

Equilibrium bid and offer prices for ABC stock can be determined if one further piece of information is known – the percentage of participants who are bulls (denoted by k) and the percentage of participants who are bears (denoted by $1 - k$). In this simplified setting, the divergence of expectations among participants has two dimensions: (1) the magnitude of the difference between the high and the low valuations (in our case, \$30 – \$20) and (2) the distribution of investors between the two valuations (as represented by k). The value of ABC's stock will therefore fall somewhere between \$20 and \$30 depending on the value of k. For example, if half of all traders are bullish ($k = .50$), then the equilibrium price should be \$25 (i.e., .50 × \$30 plus .50 × \$20 = \$25).

How do participants know or find out about the value of k? The primary way is by observing the orders that are sent to the financial market. These orders are created in response to news about ABC's prospects as well as overall macroeconomic conditions. Thus, participants discover the value of k through the orders that are revealed as trading progresses. As these trades are reported for everyone to see, the price of ABC shares fluctuates in response to changing beliefs about k.

In actual markets, participants' divergent expectations are distributed over a wider range of valuations, and we cannot refer simply to one variable, k. Nevertheless, the conclusion still holds – when expectations are divergent, prices must be discovered through the trading process in financial markets. The process is not simple and can be messy and protracted at times as investors sort through a multitude of signals from both the financial markets and the macroeconomy, many of which might be conflicting.

3.4 The Various Types of Financial Markets

As discussed in the limit order book example of the Finance chapter, a thin, illiquid financial market imposes higher transaction costs on investors and can deter some participants from placing orders in the first place. For example, in an illiquid limit order book market (also referred to as a continuous "order-driven" market), an information shock can cause a sudden surge in orders to buy or sell, and this might result in a wider bid-ask spread. If no new bids and offers enter the limit order book, then the bid-ask spread that investors must pay will be much higher, and thus, it will become more expensive to trade a company's stock. In addition, this higher spread can lead to greater price volatility because even if the best bid and ask quotes remain constant, transaction prices will bounce between the bid and offer due to the intermittent arrival of market orders to sell against the lower bid and market orders to buy against the much higher offer. This effect is commonly referred to as the "bid-ask bounce," and this bounce contributes to short-term price volatility.

Stock prices also become more volatile in a thin order book due to "market impact," which occurs when a large buy order pushes the execution price above the best offer or a large sell order pushes the price below the best bid. When market impact is sizable, price volatility is increased because prices will then typically revert to levels observed just before the large market order was placed. Price discovery could also be more difficult in a thin market, and if so, this too would contribute to price volatility.

Consequently, a thin order book can make price discovery more difficult which, in turn, leads to less informative signals about how investors are reacting to news regarding the macroeconomy and the financial health of a specific stock such as ABC. Thus, the signals from an illiquid financial market are "noisier" than those generated by a deep, liquid market. In the extreme case, a very illiquid financial market that is buffeted by frequent information shocks leads to unreliable signals from investors, and the interactive feedback loop between the macroeconomy and financial market becomes broken. This outcome is a negative one for all parties because investors, business executives, and policymakers no longer have freely flowing information about how their actions are affecting both the macroeconomy and financial markets. Consequently, illiquidity can stymie economic growth and undermine the returns offered by stocks and bonds.

Beyond the limit order book, or continuous order-driven, market structure described in the Finance chapter, there are two other primary ways to organize a financial market: (1) a periodic call auction and (2) a dealer market (also known as a "quote-driven" market). A call auction is a periodic (as opposed to a continuous) order-driven market. These alternative market structures can help large buyers and sellers that might otherwise be reluctant to enter their orders into a quote-driven continuous market. These traders are reluctant to submit large orders because of the fear of unduly pushing prices up or down (known as market impact). Another concern for these large buyers/sellers is that other traders might find out about their orders and it might lead to trades at unfavorable prices (usually referred to as "information leakage"). Unrevealed orders are referred to as "latent liquidity."

As discussed in the Finance chapter, with a call auction, participant's orders are batched together for simultaneous execution at a single clearing price at a pre-announced point in time. When the market is called, all buy orders equal to and greater than the clearing price are executable, as are all sell orders equal to or less than the clearing price. Trading prices are set at values that maximize the number of shares that execute. By batching many transactions together, a call auction concentrates liquidity and, in so doing, can significantly decrease transaction costs for participants. Calls also facilitate "quantity discovery" by allowing larger orders to be executed with less market impact and reduced information leakage. The integration of revealed and latent liquidity could be better harmonized in a call auction as the latent liquidity provider would be more comfortable with revealing the orders.

Why? For one reason: he/she can get price improvement, whereas, with exceptions, this does not happen with continuous order-driven trading.

In contrast to a call auction, in a dealer market, dealers (also called "market makers") state the prices at which public customers can buy or sell shares. A dealer posts two-sided quotes: a bid quote at which the market maker will buy shares if a customer is looking to sell and an ask quote at which the market maker will sell shares if a customer is looking to buy. As noted earlier, a dealer market is commonly referred to as a quote-driven market. The primary benefit of a dealer market is that it can provide immediacy by allowing public buyers and sellers to interact directly and quickly with a dealer so that these public customers face less risk of not having their orders executed (referred to as "execution risk"). Thus, a dealer market can reduce execution risk, but this usually comes with a trade-off in terms of wider bid-ask spreads and less transparency about other buyers and sellers in the market.

In addition to order-driven continuous markets, quote-driven markets, and periodic call auctions, other mechanisms exist to meet more specialized trading needs. For example, a block trading mechanism is used to handle the sizable orders of large investors (typically institutional) who are trying to limit the adverse impact of their large orders on the prices they wind up trading at. A large order, typically defined as an order for 10,000 shares or more, can be negotiated either person to person (face to face or via telephone or instant message) or executed via an electronic interface.

As new technology has emerged, financial markets and investor trading strategies continue to evolve. For example, relatively new trading mechanisms that allow orders to trade without publicly disclosing their trading interests are called "dark pools." Dark pools are private trading forums as opposed to trading that takes place on public exchanges like the New York Stock Exchange and Nasdaq. These mechanisms are so named to emphasize their lack of transparency compared to "lit" public exchanges. While dark pools came about primarily to facilitate block trading by institutional investors, they are now used for trading of both small- and large-sized orders. Small retail orders received by large brokerage houses can be executed internally, without being sent to public exchanges, and this too is considered a form of dark pool trading.

Dark pools are so-called dark to distinguish them from "lit" markets. Public stock exchanges are considered lit because of their higher levels of order book transparency. The following applies: (1) price discovery typically takes place through trading in public exchanges; (2) these prices are then used for trading in the dark pools; and (3) dark pools enhance quantity discovery, particularly for the large participants who, otherwise, are reluctant to send their orders to lit markets. The growing separation of price discovery and quantity discovery is not, however, without drawbacks. Efficient values for price and quantity are better attained when the two variables are determined simultaneously. Interestingly, the two are determined simultaneously in call auction trading.

Given the competing market structure models described above, you might ask: which one is the best one to use for trading? As in many things, the answer is "it depends" on what a customer needs. Since different types of traders (e.g., retail versus institutional) have different needs, it is not surprising that exchanges and other trading venues now offer multiple market structure models in a "hybrid" format. For example, major international stock exchanges typically open and close trading with a call auction, and some have intraday auctions. Batching orders in a multilateral call auction trading system facilitates order handling, sharpens price discovery, and enhances market transparency. Call auctions do not provide immediacy, but trading in the continuous market does. The immediacy offered by a continuous market that directly follows an opening call is immensely appealing to market participants. Hence, a hybrid market structure that combines continuous trading and call auctions offers significant advantages. Furthermore, when under severe stress, price discovery breaks down in the continuous market, trading is halted, and the market is re-opened with a call auction.

Regardless of the specific structure of a financial market, the Fed and other observers of the economy need to pay attention to the liquidity of these financial markets. Investors in these trading venues not only react to signals from the Fed but also produce their own signals of investors' views of the macroeconomy via their trading patterns. Thus, price fluctuations in the bond and stock markets are used by the Fed and the U.S. Treasury to see if their expansionary and contractionary actions are having the proper effect on the economy and to assess investor reactions to the policies they announce. This simultaneous relationship between the actions of investors, business executives, and policymakers creates a tightly linked system that can allocate scarce economic resources more efficiently to create a well-functioning and productive macroeconomy. As noted earlier, this linkage between the "real world" and the "financial world" depends crucially on the liquidity of financial markets, as provided by the various market structures we have just presented.

3.5 Example of an Information Shock Based on the Fed's Actions and the Financial Market's Reactions

To illustrate some economic-related information shocks and the interplay between the economy and financial markets, we can examine how the Fed's statements by Chairman Jerome Powell in early October 2018 about possible further Federal Funds rate hikes caused a sharp drop in equities during the fourth quarter of 2018. The S&P 500 stock market index fell 14.0% between the end of September 2019 and the end of December 2019. The swift and sharp negative reaction by the stock and bond markets to Powell's unexpected statement that there is "a long way to go" before further rate increases would stop prompted the Fed chairman to declare in early January 2019 that the Fed will instead show "patience" in terms of any further rate increases. The stock market immediately rallied +3.4% on the day of Powell's comments about a slower approach to Federal Funds rate increases. The Fed held rates steady for most of 2019 and then actually started lowering interest rates during August–November 2019. Three successive 0.25% cuts to the Federal Funds rate decreased it from a range of 2.0–2.5% in the summer of 2019 to 1.50–1.75% by November 2019. The Fed referred to this change from contractionary to expansionary monetary policy as a "mid-cycle adjustment" given concerns about a possible

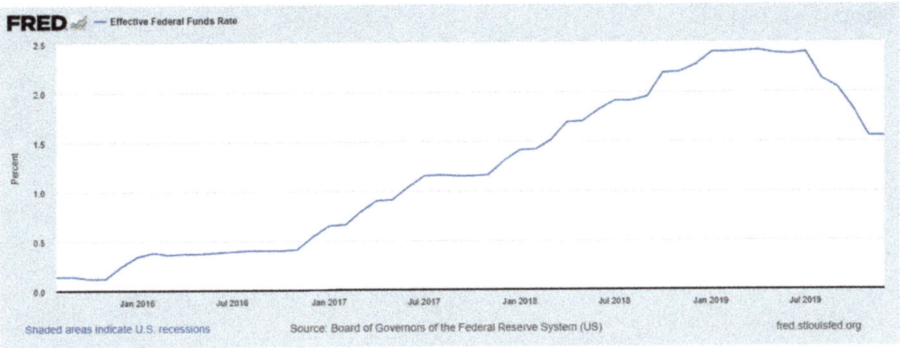

Exhibit 3.1 Federal funds rate history (2015–2019)

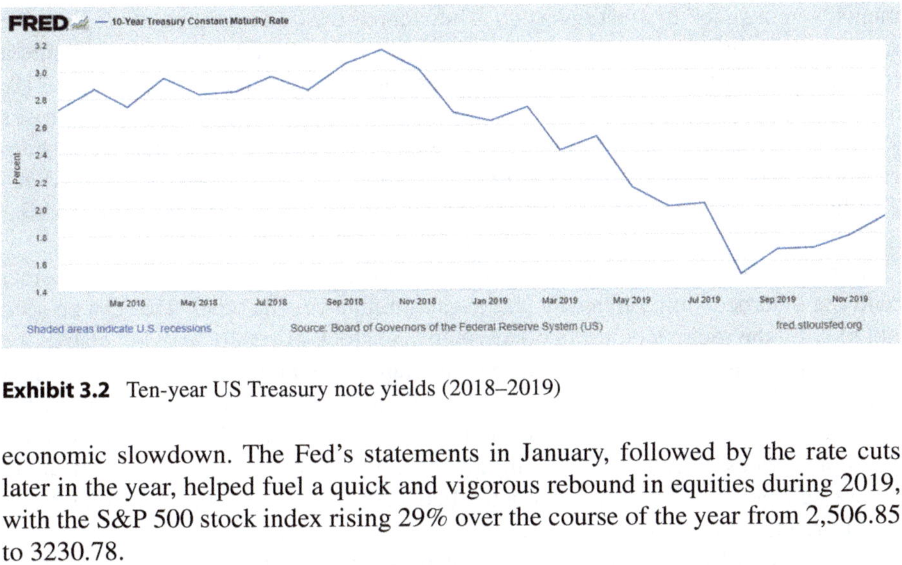

Exhibit 3.2 Ten-year US Treasury note yields (2018–2019)

economic slowdown. The Fed's statements in January, followed by the rate cuts later in the year, helped fuel a quick and vigorous rebound in equities during 2019, with the S&P 500 stock index rising 29% over the course of the year from 2,506.85 to 3230.78.

The sequence of events described above represents a clear example of the continuous feedback loop between the macroeconomy and financial markets. Presented below are some graphs and news items related to the events that unfolded during October 2018–December 2019.

The unexpected news first revealed by Fed Chairman Powell's statement in early October 2018 was quoted by CNBC.com as follows: "We [i.e., the Fed] may go neutral, but we're a long way from neutral at this point, probably." This statement was made after the Fed had already raised the Federal Funds rate nine times, starting in December 2015. Powell's statement was a surprise because many analysts and

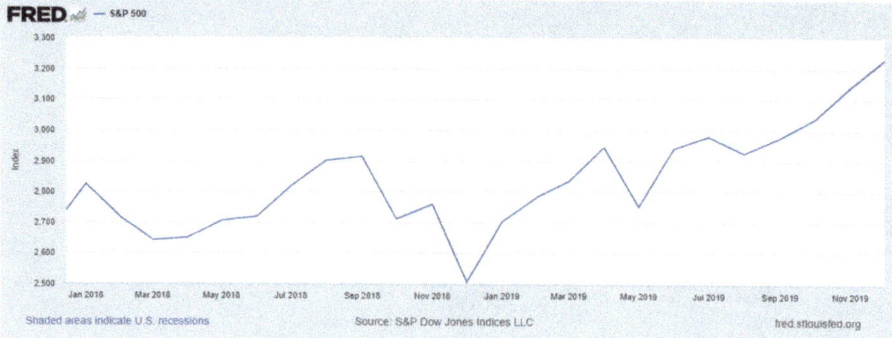

Exhibit 3.3 S&P 500 stock market index longer-term movements (2018–2019)

financial market participants had thought that a Federal Funds rate of 2.5% was sufficient to maintain strong economic growth while keeping inflation in check. Exhibit 3.1 shows the path of this key interest rate during August 2015–December 2019.

Given the market's expectations in early October 2018, the Fed chairman's statements were a shock to most investors. They feared the Fed might be too aggressive in its contractionary monetary policy and could eventually push the economy into a recession. Accordingly, 10-year U.S. Treasury note yields initially jumped to 3.21% after the announcement before falling to 2.69% by the end of 2018, while stocks sank 14% throughout the fourth quarter. Fears of a recession prompted these sharp reactions and created a great deal of price volatility in bond and stock markets. Exhibit 3.2 shows the path of Treasury note yields during 2018–2019, and Exhibit 3.3 displays the S&P 500 stock market index over this time period.

Exhibits 3.2 and 3.3 provide vivid illustrations of how financial markets interact with the macroeconomy in a way where each influences the other. This can be seen not only by the rapid declines in bond yields and stock prices in 2018 but also in the positive responses to the Fed's subsequent statements and actions in 2019 to first pause and then ultimately lower the Federal Funds rate. After initially spooking the financial markets in 2018, the Fed's actions sparked major rallies in both the stock and bond prices during 2019.[3] Along the way, market participants were constantly assessing any new information about the Fed's tendencies, and the Fed itself closely monitored the market's reactions to its changes in monetary policy.

We can also "zoom in" to examine how the stock market reacted to the Fed chairman's comments by looking at the intraday prices surrounding the specific dates of these statements. Intraday price movements on October 3–5, 2018, for the S&P 500 are presented below.

As one can see from Exhibit 3.4, there is a strong and swift reaction to Chairman Powell's surprise comments about the need for further interest rate increases. Notice

[3] Note that bond prices move inversely with interest rate changes, so the dramatic decline in the 10-year U.S. Treasury note yield from over 3.2% in October 2018 to 1.5% in August 2019 generated large capital gains for bond investors.

Exhibit 3.4 S&P 500 stock market index intraday movements (October 3, 2018–October 5, 2018)

that the reaction began during the afternoon of October 3rd right after the chairman's comments were made public (highlighted in the graph by the oval). When markets are informationally efficient, we expect this type of quick reaction to unexpected news. As shown below in Exhibit 3.5 for a single day, the initial fall was immediate and steep (a 0.4% drop from the market's peak at 2:15 pm to the close at 4:00 pm on October 3); the market's sell-off continued during October 4–5 for a total decline of 1.8% from its pre-announcement peak as market participants fully processed the implications of possible continued interest rate hikes on the economy and financial markets.[4] By zooming in further, we can see by the circle in Exhibit 3.5 that most of the initial reaction in the S&P 500 occurred between 2:15 pm and 2:55pm. This type of pattern commonly occurs when the financial market's initial response is swift and strong, but as the earlier graph in Exhibit 3.4 shows, the trend in prices can continue for several days as the process of harmonizing divergent expectations through trading plays out between "bulls" and "bears."

In contrast to the stock market's behavior in October 2018 shown above, we can also consider another sharp and rapid reaction, but now in the opposite direction for the S&P 500 index. As noted earlier, the market responded positively to Powell's more conciliatory comments related to putting potential future rate increases on

[4] If this decline over 2+ days were annualized, the cumulative loss would be approximately 84% of an investor's original value after 1 year.

Exhibit 3.5 S&P 500 stock market index intraday movements (October 3, 2018)

hold early in 2019. This reaction can be seen in Exhibit 3.6 by the intraday price patterns for this major stock index during January 3–4, 2019.

Exhibit 3.6 shows a large jump during the early morning on January 4, 2019 (see the first oval in the graph). The initial positive reaction at the market's 9:30 am open was due to a surprisingly robust nonfarm employment report released earlier that morning at 8:30 am which showed 312,000 jobs were created in the United States during December 2018. Once the stock market reopened at 9:30 am on January 4, the S&P 500 stock index surged to 2475.90 (a 1.1% increase from the prior day's close of 2447.89). This large, discontinuous jump from the previous closing price is referred to as a "gap up" in the parlance of technical analysis (which is discussed in the final section of this chapter). This is a classic example of how financial markets respond quickly to unexpected positive news about the macroeconomy.

The stock market then jumped a second time later that morning between 10:00 am and 11:00 am because Chairman Powell stated that the Fed was contemplating putting future Federal Funds rate increases on hold. Like the pattern shown earlier in Exhibits 3.4 and 3.5, the chairman's public comments about monetary policy were unexpected, and thus, traders and investors responded quickly, as can be seen by the second oval shown in Exhibit 3.6. The net effect on stock prices was swift and sizable. The index then continued to trend up over the rest of the day and closed at 2531.94 for a total gain of 3.02% from the prior day's close. This represents a large gain because U.S. stock market indexes typically fluctuate less than 1% on a daily basis.

Exhibit 3.7 shows how differences in the liquidity of individual securities can affect the price discovery process around Chairman Powell's comments on January 4, 2019. To illustrate how two stocks can react in very different ways to the same news from the Fed chairman, Exhibit 3.7 shows the intraday price patterns from 9:30 am to 11:15 am on that day for a very liquid stock, Microsoft (a global software giant), and a fairly illiquid stock, Flushing Financial (a small commercial bank

Exhibit 3.6 S&P 500 Stock Market Index Intraday Movements (January 3, 2019–January 4, 2019)

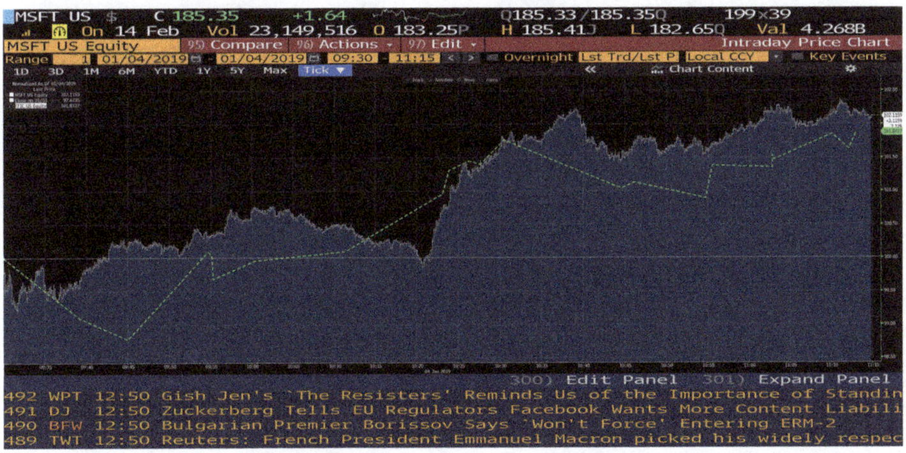

Exhibit 3.7 Large versus small cap stocks' intraday movements (January 4, 2019)

based in New York City). The white line traces the fluctuations for Microsoft stock, while the dashed line displays the movements in Flushing Financial.[5] Notice that Microsoft's price pattern is much smoother because trades occur frequently and at

[5] Both stocks have been indexed to a starting baseline value of 100 to facilitate comparison.

prices that are fairly close to prior prices. So despite the major news from the Fed that day, Microsoft's stock responds quickly and in a "fair and orderly" manner because many trades were being executed within every minute of trading.

In contrast, the dashed line of Flushing Financial moves in an abrupt, jagged way because its stock does not trade that frequently. This also leads the stock's price to lag behind movements in the S&P 500 stock index and Microsoft. In fact, during the 9:30–11:15 am period on this day, Flushing Financial's stock traded only 25 times, while Microsoft traded 2,520 times! In addition, the total daily share trading volume was 44,061,000 for Microsoft and only 67,250 for Flushing Financial.

This represents a very large difference in trading activity, with Microsoft's stock exhibiting much greater liquidity, as buyers and sellers can easily trade at any time during the trading (e.g., 24 times per minute on average). In contrast, Flushing Financial's stock does not trade very often over this time period (once every 4.2 minutes), and thus, its price must move more sharply when it does eventually trade in order to "catch up" to news about the U.S. jobs report and the Fed chairman's comments. Thus, discovering the "correct" price for an illiquid stock like Flushing Financial is much more difficult because of the lack of frequent trades. Although this graph shows only two stocks, these differences in liquidity exist across the thousands of stocks that trade in the United States on any given day.

The trading mechanics and price discovery process described earlier in this chapter were the primary instruments needed to facilitate these interactions between the macroeconomy and financial markets. Thus, it is important to have well-functioning, liquid financial markets to make the signals between policymakers, investors, business executives, and consumers as clear as possible.

3.6 Using the TraderEx Simulation to Understand Interactions Between Financial Markets and the Macroeconomy

The TraderEx trading simulation system is an excellent way to demonstrate and "bring to life" the concepts described thus far in this book about liquidity and market structure. Specifically, this chapter focuses on the interactions between financial markets and the macroeconomy. TraderEx can be played among multiple players in a "network session" environment or in a "solitaire session" mode against the computer. It accommodates the three main types of markets (order-driven, quote-driven, and call auction). More details on how to operate the TraderEx system can be found in Chapter 5, Experiencing Market Dynamics with TraderEx: A Trading Decision-Making Simulation. In this section here, we focus on how the concept of information shocks can be brought to life via the TraderEx system.

One can incorporate information shocks related to macroeconomic news into the simulation either by having the instructor provide brief, unexpected "news items" within the system for everyone to see or by simply announcing the information aloud to all players. A variant on this type of game play would be for the instructor to provide this macroeconomic news privately to only a select few participants in order to simulate "an informed trader" environment where some players have an information advantage over other participants. For example, one could first provide news privately about an impending positive U.S. employment report to the proprietary traders and then announce this news publicly to the rest of the players in the class later in the simulation. Similarly, news about a sudden change in the Federal Funds rate could be shared privately at first or announced publicly to everyone at the same time.

If the players are acting in an efficient way, then one would expect those with private information to place market orders to buy when the news is positive and to place market orders to sell when the news is negative. In addition, divergent expectations can lead some informed traders to buy, while other informed investors decide to sell. Either way, the informed players can quickly take advantage of their informational edge. Attentive buy-side traders that are uninformed could also adjust their limit orders based on a sudden surge in market orders by informed traders. For example, those uninformed traders with a buy mission might cancel their existing buy orders and enter new orders at higher bid prices if they fear that there are many market buy orders by informed traders that will quickly push prices upward. To increase the likelihood of getting their orders executed, these uninformed investors will want to raise their bids to be more in sync with the sudden jump in transaction prices caused by the informed traders' actions. Those uninformed investors with a sell mission might follow a similar approach by canceling their original orders and placing new sell orders at a higher limit price. The reverse would be true for these buy-side traders if the news was negative and many market sell orders by informed traders have flooded in (i.e., uninformed traders would cancel the original orders and replace them with lower bid and ask prices to increase their chances of getting their orders filled). By carefully observing the trading activity, the uninformed participants can infer a great deal about the informed traders' private knowledge which can then lead to better price discovery and improved market efficiency.

After reviewing the TraderEx results, it is usually best to re-run the simulation with each player trying the role of a different type of trader (e.g., a market maker can become a buy-side trader or informed trader in the second round of game play and so on). In this way, one can get a sense of how different objectives can affect the way a trader reacts to macroeconomic news and how traders will handle their orders to achieve specific goals.

3.7 Making the Trade: Combining Macroeconomics with Fundamental Analysis and Technical Analysis

The final point we consider in this chapter is how an investor can use the concepts we have presented to make effective investments in a real-world financial market such as the New York Stock Exchange or Nasdaq. Economists and other market participants also need to understand an investor's perspective in order to anticipate how economic policies and conditions can impact the liquidity of financial markets and how these markets can influence interest rates and the macroeconomy.

Since macroeconomic conditions can appreciably affect the future cash flows for a stock, investors must be attuned to the trends in key economic indicators. For example, investors typically monitor the growth in real gross domestic product (GDP), employment and wages, business investment, personal consumption, corporate profits, as well as changes in interest rates, inflation, and productivity, to name a few of the economy's major variables. In addition, as demonstrated in a prior section, one must understand and follow changes in a government's monetary and fiscal policies because they can have profound effects on the economy in general and on financial markets in particular. An investor interested, for example, in buying the stock of a hypothetical company called ABC would like to see that the economy is operating in a "virtuous cycle" where employment and wage growth is strong because this will encourage increased consumption by consumers which, in turn, translates into increased sales and profits for corporations. The greater prosperity of consumers and businesses will then typically spur increased investment by these businesses which can lead them to hire more employees and pay them higher wages. This sets off another stage of greater consumption by consumers and further economic growth. In the ideal case, this virtuous cycle continues without triggering increases in inflation and interest rates. If inflation and interest rates start to rise, then the Fed and other policymakers must decide whether contractionary monetary and fiscal policy is called for to cool down the economy before it "overheats."

Conversely, a "vicious" economic cycle can set in if consumers suddenly stop spending as much as in the past, possibly due to concerns about the future political climate and economic conditions. This can lead to lower sales and corporate profits, less business investment, and ultimately employee layoffs, which can then reinforce consumers' concerns, causing them to spend even less, which leads to a further decline in corporate profits. In this case, the economy becomes mired in a negative cycle where conditions continue to deteriorate, and the economy falls into a recession. As that point approaches, the Fed and other government policymakers must decide whether expansionary monetary and fiscal policies are needed to stimulate the economy and break this negative cycle.

The above discussion reveals the importance of first understanding the country's macroeconomic conditions to decide how much one should be invested in the stock market at the current time. If economic conditions are good, then investing more in the stock market is a viable option, and so the next step is to evaluate various sectors of the economy to see which might perform the best in the near future.[6] For example, auto manufacturers tend to do well as an economy emerges from a recession, while technology stocks typically perform best in the middle of an economic expansion. In contrast, consumer product companies such as food producers and utility companies tend to outperform at the end of an economic expansion and the beginning of a recession. This "rotation" between different industries, or economic sectors, requires the investor to be aware of current trends in the business cycle.

[6]The approach we focus on here is commonly referred to as a "top down" investment style. In contrast, some investors prefer to use a "bottom-up" approach where the prospects of individual companies are first analyzed, and the macroeconomic conditions are of secondary importance.

Having identified current economic conditions and which sectors are likely to perform well, an investor can then perform "fundamental analysis" to identify which stock(s) to buy. This analysis typically requires that the investor study the firm's trends in growth, profitability, and risk-taking. Ideally, an investor should select a firm that has strong growth, consistently high profitability, and a relatively low risk business model. A good fundamental analysis would also entail estimating a firm's fundamental or "intrinsic value" by forecasting future cash flows and discounting these flows using a cost of capital that is commensurate with the firm's riskiness. In this way, an investor can determine if his/her estimate of the firm's fundamental value is greater than the firm's current price observed in the stock market. If so, then the stock is trading at a cheap price relative to its intrinsic value and should be considered for purchase. For example, if an investor thinks ABC is worth $30 per share and the current stock price is only $25, then the investor can make a $5 dollar profit if other market participants eventually realize that the firm should be valued at this higher price.

An investor might also want to consider one final aspect before placing a limit or market order to buy ABC stock at $25 per share. That is, after identifying a potentially profitable investment in ABC, some investors will also perform "technical analysis" to see if this is the right time to buy the stock. For example, if ABC's stock price has been trending down over the past 3 months, an investor might want to use technical analysis to determine whether this short-term trend will continue. If this trend does continue, then the investor is actually better off to wait for the price to decrease further in the near future so that he/she can buy ABC for even lower than $25 per share (in which case, the profit will be greater when the price rebounds and ultimately climbs to the investor's projected price of $30).

However, for past price patterns to be useful, one needs to know whether financial markets are informationally efficient and thus conform to the "efficient market hypothesis" (EMH) discussed in the Finance chapter. In our context, if information shocks cannot be predicted and financial markets are perfectly efficient, then past prices are not of any help either in the short or long term. In such a market, stock price changes are uncorrelated, and price moves resemble a "random walk" pattern.

Have the random walk and the EMH been validated? From our perspective on trading, the most relevant tests of the EMH are based on very short period, intraday data; and the tests have shown that intraday correlation patterns do indeed exist, thus rejecting the EMH – at least over short time intervals. On any given day, both positive and negative intraday correlation patterns exist in complex combinations. The patterns also continuously evolve, and so exploiting them with technical analysis or any other tools is far from an easy task. Nevertheless, astute traders recognize and deal with these realities when implementing their investment decisions.

Technical analysis uses the recent history of stock prices and trading volume to predict future stock values and, in this case, might identify a short-term price "bottom" of, say, $22 per share for ABC's stock. So an investor would use this short-term forecast to wait until ABC's price dropped to $22, with a goal of placing a limit buy order at this price point. If the investor is correct in both the technical and fundamental analyses, then the purchase order will execute at $22, and the gain from the trade will be greater at $8 per share ($30 - $22) rather than the $5 per share profit based solely on fundamental analysis.

Although this is not the place where we could possibly do justice to all of the details and nuances of technical analysis, one example of this technique is the use of a simple "cross-over" strategy where a price bottom can be identified when the current price rises above a moving average of past prices (e.g., the price rises to $22 when the 65-day moving average is $21).[7] This cross-over suggests that prices will now continue on an upswing because the new price of $22 has broken the old pattern of lower prices at $21. Clearly, there are many different types of technical analysis patterns (typically referred to as "studies"), and it can take several years for a person to become an expert in all of them. In response to this proliferation of technical studies, computerized trading algorithms have also been created to help automate and sharpen this type of analysis. This complexity of trading patterns is consistent with our view that price discovery is a difficult, protracted process that involves runs and reversals that might be detected by technical analysis and dealt with via sophisticated trading algorithms.

3.8 Wrapping Up: How Information Shocks Affect Financial Markets and the Economy

Market participants can benefit greatly from knowing how the macroeconomy and financial markets interact with each other. For example, a deeper understanding of the prominent role of macroeconomic-related information shocks could help one identify via fundamental analysis which industries (and what firms within those sectors) will perform well in the future. In addition, the specific timing and placement of trades could be enhanced if effective technical analysis techniques are employed. By employing the concepts and analytical tools described in this chapter, financial assets can be assessed more accurately, and the financial markets' signals to the macroeconomy will be clearer, thus benefiting society.

It should also be noted that the 2020 COVID-19 pandemic offers another vivid illustration of how the economy and stock market can react to an information shock. In this case, the information shock was "exogenous" to the macroeconomy and financial markets (i.e., it originated outside of the economy due to the rapid global spread of the novel coronavirus in 2019–2020). As economies and societies around the world were "locked down" to halt the virus's spread, the economic and financial effects were immediate and severe. In the United States, the unemployment rate went from record lows to historic highs within a matter of months during the first half of 2020. Due to this health crisis-induced shock to the economy, investors quickly sold stocks and sought the safety of U.S. Treasury securities, both of

[7] Conversely, a cross-over strategy to sell a stock would occur when the current price falls below a moving average of past prices. Please note that in this section, we neither support nor deny the validity of technical analysis, but only note that it is being used today by many traders. Our intention here is to give you a quick sense of what is involved with this widely used technique.

which pushed stock prices and Treasury yields down. In turn, governments quickly intervened with monetary and fiscal stimulus to soften the powerful blow to the economy and to provide time for scientists to come up with therapeutics and ultimately a vaccine. As the drama unfolded, the stock market whipsawed between gut-wrenching plunges and sharp upswings, while intraday volatility surged to record highs in the United States and elsewhere. The driving force for these sudden movements was the nature of the information about the growing pandemic. This virus-related news was often complex, conflicting, and, in many cases, quite unreliable. Consequently, investor expectations were extremely divergent, and this no doubt added to the substantial surge in short-term price volatility. The violent market fluctuations during the first half of 2020 are another dramatic example of how financial markets and the economy interact with each other in the face of unexpected news.

4 Trading and Technology: An Information Systems Course Application

Chapter 1 focuses on microeconomics. In it we present the Capital Asset Pricing Model (CAPM), a theoretical formulation that shows, without reference to a "real-world" marketplace where shares are traded, how prices are set in a frictionless, zero trading cost environment. At the end of Chapter 1, we introduce friction in a minimalistic way and show that doing so perturbs market outcomes. In Chap. 2, which focuses on finance, we go deeper into the realities of price determination and trading in a non-frictionless environment. In so doing, we show that the structure of a marketplace does indeed matter. In this chapter, we drill down and examine the capabilities IT provides. We examine the realities of a non-frictionless market in order to focus on how technology can enhance the efficiency of an actual marketplace. Difficult market design issues arise when an actual computerized trading mechanism is developed and operated. As IT professionals know, a production system is a big step forward from a conceptual design or a prototype. That is the direction in which we now head.

Technology has transformed trading and provided new computerized marketplaces that bring buyers and sellers of securities together efficiently and transparently. Gone are loud trading floors and a flurry of paper tickets to process. Today, software mediates the submission and prioritization of buy and sell orders, and stock exchange matching engines facilitate trades with millisecond timing. Most trading orders are now submitted by software using complex algorithms that respond to live market data. Computer technologies underpin the essential functioning of today's markets from price dissemination, to order matching, to the clearing and settling of trades.

Banking institutions, innovators, and entrepreneurs continually develop new systems and technologies to meet the needs of traders and to enhance the operations of markets. Most recently, Distributed Ledger Technology (DLT) and Blockchain applications,[1] more than could previously be imagined, offer exciting opportunities

[1] A blockchain is a data structure (i.e., data in a predefined format) used in distributed ledgers that store and transmit packages of data called "blocks" that are "chained" together. A distributed ledger shares blockchain data across a network of computers accessed by different network partici-

D. Ozenbas et al., *Liquidity, Markets and Trading in Action*, Classroom Companion: Business, https://doi.org/10.1007/978-3-030-74817-3_4

to radically change the operations of markets and widen access to trading venues and the safe settlement of transactions.

This chapter covers the foundational technologies that have been implemented (1) to create end user trading systems and online markets and (2) to computerize financial operations. Three key technologies – application software, database systems, and networks – power trading today, and participants in financial markets must understand them and their roles in supporting successful trading operations. Moreover, these technologies are often applied to create innovative market systems that are not merely incremental improvements to current practice, but that fundamentally disrupt the industry and establish new, leading firms. Think of how the ride-sharing firms Uber and Lyft have used IT and ubiquitous smartphones to disrupt the taxi and limousine industries and offer innovative new services.

Information systems students and skilled technology developers will have many types of jobs and career paths open to them in trading and the financial markets industry. They could be doing work for an active trading desk performing tasks that range from customizing software and collaborating with market data vendors to connectivity to the many data sources and market venues relied on today. Start-up ventures also need IS professionals to develop novel systems that revolutionize how a financial process (e.g., consolidating data and analyzing risk) is carried out to launch a new system to improve price discovery for difficult-to-trade securities. This chapter will be useful for information systems (I.S.) classes that emphasize applications of technology in banking or capital markets, or for a finance course that examines the technology operations and management challenges in a high tech industry such as the finance sector.

4.1 IT Innovations: Disruptive Versus Incremental

Innovations in the financial markets that are *disruptive* lead to new entrants challenging incumbent organizations and to a reordering of the players in the industry. An example is Nasdaq, which launched in the United States in 1971 as the first fully automated stock market. Its initial goal was to automate the daily "pink sheets" of indicative (non-firm) bid and ask quotes of small, over-the-counter stocks. Within several years, Nasdaq grew to rival the New York Stock Exchange (NYSE), in particular attracting the initial public offerings (IPOs) of many growth and technology stocks such as Apple (1980), Microsoft and Adobe (both 1986) and Dell (1988), that remained Nasdaq stocks in defiance of the existing Wall Street convention of listings moving to the more prestigious "Big Board" as soon as a company qualified for an NYSE listing.

pants. Until recently ledgers were centralized and held by a controlling entity. Distributed Ledger Technology (DLT) is the set of approaches to recording and sharing data across multiple ledgers or data stores. DLT could have applications in securities market infrastructure and allow for transactions and data to be recorded and synchronized across a distributed network. Blockchains were first widely applied as the underlying technology of the cryptocurrency Bitcoin.

While disruptors like Nasdaq can displace established, market-leading institutions (OTC pink sheets) and capture market share from incumbent organizations, other technology innovations are *incremental* and support the business models of established firms or markets. The NYSE, for instance, developed its designated order turnaround (DOT) system for electronically routing small market orders of up to 2,000 shares to the trading floor in 1976. DOT expanded the market's capacity but retained the roles of NYSE floor traders. A second example is the launch in 1977 of the Society for Worldwide Interbank Financial Telecommunications (SWIFT) messaging service. Developed cooperatively by six major international banks, SWIFT operates a system for international money and security transfers. Today, SWIFT is a vast messaging network used by banks and other financial institutions to securely send and receive information, such as money transfer instructions. Rather than disrupting international money by bypassing the major banks, the SWIFT system enhanced the services its participating banks can offer their customers.

New technology innovations such as Blockchain can be applied in either incremental, "competence-enhancing" ways or in a disruptive, "competence-destroying" way. Financial institutions that are "Goliaths" prefer the incremental use of information technology (IT) that supports or improves their market position, while start-up firms are often "Davids" that want to win customers to a radically new approach to what the incumbent firms are offering. Bitcoin and Ethereum are the two most popular cryptocurrencies in 2021. As they are more widely adopted, what disruptive consequences can you imagine for established financial organizations?

In the next section of this chapter, we outline the information technologies (IT) that underpin markets and trading systems that have enhanced market transparency and improved efficiency. The section that follows will examine the economic impacts information systems have on financial markets and trading. This chapter will finish with examples of market participants and their technology tools.

4.2 IT Infrastructure for Financial Markets

Technologists refer to the "layers" of IT that are integrated to build an information system. The lowest layer is hardware and infrastructure such as servers, telecommunications equipment such as routers and switches, and data storage devices. On top of the hardware layer are shared systems such as databases and network directories. The top layer of the stack contains applications that enable users to perform business and financial market functions. At the bottom of the stack are the physical devices that process and store financial market data and that send and receive data over telecommunications networks (Fig. 4.1).

Layers of IT Infrastructure	Example components
Applications	– Software programs – End-user and Enterprise applications – Communications applications – Analytics and modeling
Shared services and common applications	– Network connectivity – Database management systems (DBMS) – Data and network address registries
Hardware components	– Physical computer servers – Data storage devices – Network cabling and routers – Security access firewalls – Other data center devices

Fig. 4.1 A simplified three-layer IT stack. Components in each layer perform defined, self-contained functions yet interact with the other components and other layers using common standards and established communications protocols

4.3 IT Support for the Economic Functions of Financial Markets

Financial markets perform three basic economic functions: consolidate buying and selling interests, enforce market rules that ensure fairness and promote trust, and connect investors to those who need capital to fund their business or public sector initiatives (e.g., road construction). The goal of technologists working in the capital markets industry is to perform these functions as cost efficiently and profitably as possible, in many cases, using off the shelf software rather than building costly customized systems from scratch.[2] The first market function to consider is bringing together buyers and sellers of securities, currencies, and derivative contracts and providing price and trading volume information.

Before the computer era, traders gathered on "open outcry" market floors, representing buyers and sellers and following the exchange's rules to discover prices and exchange ownership and cash. This concentration of activity was beneficial for investors since it maximized the chance of finding a counterparty and trading at competitively determined prices. As open outcry trading has been replaced by screen-based markets, real-time market information that was once accessible only to those on the trading floor is now widely available. By providing trading information and a process for price discovery for standardized instruments – stocks, bonds, foreign currency, and derivative products (futures and options) – markets play an important role in facilitating buying and selling. The effects of more information dissemination and reduced latency (from a trading decision to a completed trade) have enhanced liquidity and provided more trading choices to investors than they had when floor markets dominated.

[2] Off-the-shelf or hosted software is sold by IT vendors to financial firms as a more cost-effective solution compared to customized software that a firm might build for itself.

A second function of markets is to provide formal rules for setting prices and matching orders. For instance, a market order to sell arriving to an open outcry floor market would be required to trade at the highest available bid price; otherwise, a "trade-through" violation has occurred. As discussed in Chapter 2, a superior bid price that was traded through will lead to the seller receiving an inferior price. Most electronic order book markets execute limit orders according to "price-time" priority rules (the best priced orders arriving earliest will trade first). Enforcing rules and ensuring that participants' orders are treated fairly generates trust and can be explicitly coded into the order matching software of a computerized market. In addition, conflicts of interest and opportunities for fraud arise in markets, so investors require assurance that market information is valid and reliable. For instance, many markets prohibit "spoofing."[3]

Third, markets intermediate between the sources of capital (investors) and users of capital (companies and governments) and provide liquidity. This means that, for instance, an investor managing a fund that purchases a borrowing company's bonds does not need to hold the bonds until maturity. The buyer can reverse the decision by selling the bonds back to other buyers in the market. The liquidity of financial assets makes them more valuable than other assets that cannot be readily converted into cash (e.g., jewelry and houses). As markets have become more technologically advanced, more investors are willing to invest in businesses and can sell or buy to reflect their opinions and willingness to take on risk.[4]

4.4 Instruments and Market Data

Many things of value can be traded, and open-air marketplaces, souks, and storefronts have existed since the dawn of civilization. Financial markets facilitate the transfer of money into financial instruments, which are issued or sold to investors by companies to raise capital or by government bodies to borrow funds. Traded instruments fall into several standard categories (Fig. 4.2).

Cash/spot markets	**Derivatives markets**
• Equities • Fixed income/bonds • Currencies	• Commodity futures • Financial futures • Options • Swaps • Forwards
Other markets	
• Real estate • Art, antiques, etc.	

Fig. 4.2 Traded markets by instrument type

[3] As identified in Chap. 2, "spoofing" refers to the entry of orders to create a misleading impression of supply and demand. Spoofing orders are then cancelled before they can execute.

[4] The role of intermediaries in the provision of liquidity is discussed in more detail in Chap. 2.

While a large company may manufacture many products in various sizes, colors, and configurations, its securities are standardized into a narrow range by the type of "claim" they represent for the investor. Bond are obligations and bondholder claims are prioritized over common stockholders for instance. Financial markets draw together securities, tradable instruments, investor decision-making, and a legal and operational infrastructure to support trading and trade processing.

Markets differ depending on the timing of an asset's transfer. In derivatives markets, a transaction occurs today at a set price for an asset that the purchaser (seller) may not own (deliver) until some months or years into the future.

Market systems capture and disseminate important information for market participants. Figure 4.3 shows July 7, 2021 prices of West Texas Intermediate (WTI) crude oil traded on the New York Mercantile Exchange. A contract for 1,000 barrels of oil for August 2021 delivery last traded at $71.69 per barrel. Oil futures for "back months" (further into the future) are less expensive, a situation referred to as "backwardation." Other important information is the price change since the previous day. In this display, the August 2021 contract is trading $1.68 lower than the previous closing or settlement price of $73.37. The bid and ask quotes – 71.68 and 71.70 – show what prices buyers will pay and sellers will sell at for the indicated sizes, which in the display are shown as 35 × 207 (35 contracts can be sold at the bid and 20 bought at the ask). The trading volume (863,326 contracts) and the open, high, and low prices are also disseminated along with the time of the last update of the market data (11:20 am).

In cash or spot markets, ownership of the traded instrument is transferred directly and nearly immediately. Ordinarily, at the time a futures contract expires, its price will converge to the cash price. At the time of expiration, an owner of a contract is committed to receiving the commodity according to the contract's settlement rules that

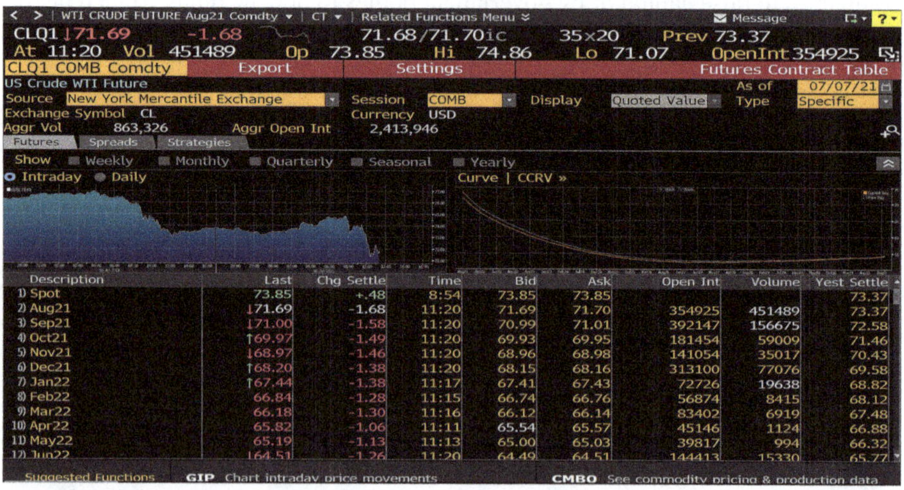

Fig. 4.3 Energy futures market – crude oil (CL) futures

Fig. 4.4 Stock quote for Google (GOOG)

specify a date and location for its delivery. In the case of the NYMEX WTI Crude Oil futures (CL), that means a pipeline or storage facility in Cushing, Oklahoma.

As shown in Fig. 4.4, shares of GOOG can be sold for $2,597.09 (bid) and bought at $2,598.43 (ask) at the time this display was live (11:22 am). Further critical information shown to traders includes the quote sizes, where 4 × 1 means that the bid quote is good for up to four round lots (400 shares) and 100 shares are offered at the ask quote. The last trade was at $2,597.77, and Val (value) shows that shares worth $783.527 million have changed hands so far this day. The day's opening trade was at $2,606.82, and the high and low of the day so far are $2,612.80 and $2,596.03, respectively.

4.5 Foundational Technologies for Trading

Three information technologies are essential in computerizing a financial market: (1) shared data files or databases on which transaction processing systems run, (2) application software to process and respond to market data, and (3) high-capacity, low-latency network technologies. The first of these, databases or data files, allows structured sets of data to be stored in a computer and to be widely accessible in various ways.

Databases and common data files underlie the critical transaction processing systems (TPSs) that provide the capabilities for online trading and the subsequent clearing and settlement of trades. A TPS for a financial market has predefined fixed inputs and outputs such as orders and executed trades and is limited to predefined operations such as entering limit orders or market orders, cancelling a limit order, and matching a buy order and a sell order to complete a trade. A TPS follows precise order execution rules and ensures that all of the updates needed to process the transaction are completed. Consider for instance, a market sell order for 1,000 shares arrives, while the best limit order to buy is good for 1,500 shares. The technology must ensure that the 1,000 share match is recorded as a trade and that the remaining 500 shares to buy remain on the order book after the trade.

The second technology is the *applications software* used by market participants. Trading software includes price and chart displays, order management systems (OMS), and algorithmic trading software that submits orders into markets according to pre-specified rules. Market software needs to be "access restricted" so that only authenticated client users with adequate capital can place orders and trade and be connected via telecoms networks to the shared servers of the market operator. The application software a trader uses today can facilitate algorithmic trading and high-frequency trading (HFT) using market price and order book signals to enter and modify orders with minimal human intervention.

The third critical technology underpinning trading activity in financial markets is *telecommunications networks*. Today, high-speed, low-latency networks carry data from market servers to users across the globe. Market data vendors such as Bloomberg, CQG, and Reuters send market information to subscribers (who are identified at the time of logging in) and can send broadcast or targeted market messages and orders. Today, networks use packet switching protocols to move data in separate, small blocks – packets – through a series of network segments to destinations whose addresses are part of each packet. When received, packets are reassembled in the proper sequence to produce the transmitted data at the end point.

The farther the distance and the more "hops" from one network segment to the next, the longer the latency or delay from transmission to receipt. To avoid such latency, HFT traders pay for "collocation services" to place their trading computers in the same data centers that house the market's computer servers. With HFT models running on their trading computers that are typically co-located in the exchange's data center, these traders are likely to be the first movers on any orders they choose to act on, or to cancel orders they submitted, before they execute.

4.6 IT Functions in Trading

The following market functions have been the focus of computerization efforts in the financial industry:

- Information systems play an *order collection* role in the processing of trading instructions in investors' and traders' offices. With an electronic system, once an order is entered, details such as size, limit price, and time are accessible for an investor's control and measurement purposes and for transmitting to a chosen market system.
- Systems for *order routing* direct an order entered by a trader to the appropriate market. The DOT system (designated order turnaround) was introduced in 1976 for order routing on the NYSE. The system enables NYSE member firms to electronically route market orders and limit orders from their offices anywhere to the specialist post on the market floor, bypassing the floor broker's booth. By 1992, 78% of NYSE orders were arriving via DOT. At that time, the remainder arrived via phone calls to floor traders' booths.

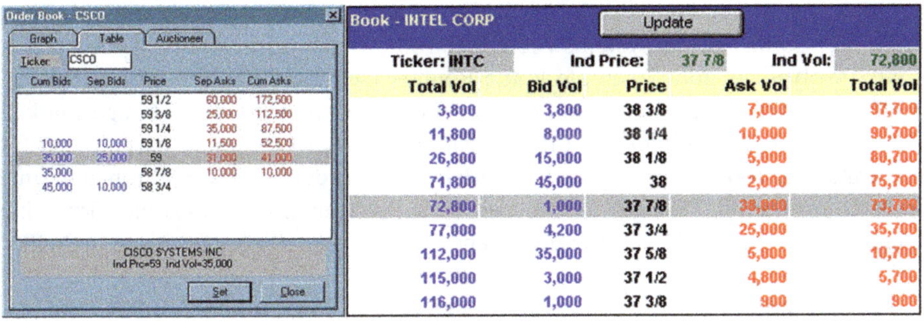

Fig. 4.5 Call auction price discovery in Cisco and Intel stock in the AZX call auction mechanism that operated from 1990 to 2001. Buyers and sellers will be matched at the shaded prices

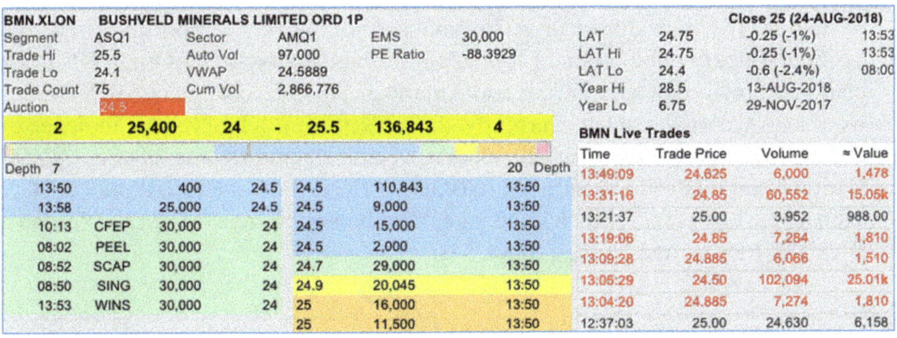

Fig. 4.6 Call auction price discovery on the London Stock Exchange. The uncrossing price will be 24.50 pence and 25,400 shares will be matched

- *Price determination* is often supported by systems that aggregate the orders submitted to a market and discover prices. The Arizona Stock Exchange (AZX) was a screen-based market for trading stocks after the daily close of New York Stock Exchange trading. The system used a single price call auction mechanism to find a price at which the maximum quantity to buy and quantity to sell can be matched. In an example from 1999 shown in Fig. 4.5, 35,000 shares of Cisco are auctioned at $59, the price that enables the greatest trade quantity to be matched. Notice that the auction is not a perfect match, as 6000 shares at $59 will remain unsold.

The London Stock Exchange (LSE) uses open, mid-day, and closing auctions to discover prices and provide added liquidity to its continuous order book system. Figure 4.6 is an example that shows a mid-day auction screen shortly before it will execute at about 14:00. The auction price is selected to be the price that enables the matching of the largest quantity of shares. In the case where there is an excess of share on one side of the market, the LSE auction executes the earliest arriving first and leaves unfilled the call auction orders that arrived later.

Order execution systems electronically match buy and sell orders in a market, and *order confirmation* systems route electronic trade verifications to the participants involved. A good example is the Reuters Dealing 2000 system launched in 1992 to electronically match buy and sell orders in the foreign exchange market. Details of executed trades are then transmitted back to the trade participants for confirmation. Today, microseconds elapse between order entry, execution, and final trade confirmation. Dealing's successor, Refinitiv, runs transactions platforms that handle an average daily volume of currency trades of nearly $500 billion in 2020.

- Systems are used for *trade reporting* and *surveillance* purposes. In the case of a fraud or market manipulation investigation, an audit trail of trades can speed investigations. The NYSE's StockWatch unit, for example, uses sophisticated software to monitor trading activities and to warn of unusual activity, which will be investigated by the staff.
- Systems *disseminate market information* more broadly. The Consolidated Tape System (CTS), introduced in 1976, imposed unified trade reporting rules and facilitated ticker publication of last sale information from any of eight US stock markets. Previously only NYSE and American Stock Exchange (AMEX) trades were reported on the ticker. Currently, the CTS informs a far broader audience of all trading activity on over 20 market venues including the NYSE, NYSE National and NYSE American, CBOE's BYX, BZX, EDGA and EDGX exchanges, Long-Term Stock Exchange, Members Exchange (MEMX), Nasdaq's BX, ISE, PHLX, and Nasdaq Stock Market.

4.7 Managing Trading Technology

A student of information systems planning to work in technology development in the financial markets industry will encounter many decisions that are no-brainers, such as upgrading software when new versions are available and changing vendors when needs change. Other decisions, such as measuring risk and setting position limits, require more thought and careful consideration, and there are strategic choices to be made with inputs from senior managers.

Speed and Reducing Latency – Nanoseconds matter for some trading strategies, but not all, depending on the investment and trading strategies being pursued by your clients. Patient trading can be beneficial and reduce costs if the holding periods of the positions are longer. Some traditional investors are concerned about the disruption and destabilization of high-frequency trading. Think of the 'flash clash' incidents (sharp price swings caused by errant trading software) that get attention when they occur. It is costly to operate a low-latency trading operation, and the optimal speed of data and order handling varies from trader to trader. Technologists need to understand how critical the timing of data transmissions is to the profitability of a strategy.

Man or Machine? – Market participants use a combination of human judgment and the rules-based logic built into customized software to manage their buy and sell orders according to their desired strategies. While market bots (robots) and algo traders capture the attention and are viewed by some as exploitive of slower human traders, the reality is more complicated. In a 2020 trial of traders accused of market manipulation, a text from one of the defendants was shared – *"As a manual trader, I can use fake bids/offers and make the algo buy/sell into my real bid/offer"* – suggesting that sometimes bot trading is less effective.[5]

A trading algorithm's effectiveness is a function of the people who developed it and the extent to which the historical data, which it was tested on, is consistent with conditions in the markets in the future. Even with their statistical sophistication, most algorithmic trading software has "kill switches" to revert to human trading judgment under extreme market conditions.

Dark or Light? – Traders typically want transparency for everyone else's orders but want to keep their own orders hidden. A disadvantage of trading in a "lit" transparent market is that simply knowing that a large order to sell (buy) is being worked through the market will put downward (upward) pressure on prices. As a result, traders in screen-based markets often choose to use hidden or "iceberg" orders or to trade in dark pools to keep their trading intentions from leaking out into the market (Fig. 4.7).

	Open "Lit" Order Book	Hidden/Iceberg Orders	Dark Pool Orders
Order placement	Enter two limit orders to sell 25,000 at $75 and $75.05	Enter a limit order to sell 50,000 at $75. Display only 10,000 in the order book with the remainder an iceberg order that will appear 10,000 shares at a time after the displayed order trades.	Enter a order to sell 50,000 into a dark pool with an indicator indicating willingness to be matched at the mid-point of the bid-ask quotes.
Possible consequences	Responding to selling pressure, the bid is cancelled, a new offer at $74.95 arrives, and the new quotes are $74.90-$74.95	The smaller displayed sell order will not trigger a price drop and buy orders arrive and fill the displayed and hidden portion of the order	A order to buy 50,000 shares or more is in the dark pool and is matched at the $75 midpoint
Possible outcome	Shares are sold for less than $75	Shares sell for $75 after some time passed and buy orders arrive	Shares sell for $75

Fig. 4.7 Example order handling approaches for a trader seeking to sell 50,000 shares of a $75 stock. The current bid and ask quotes are 74.95 and 75.05 and are good for 10,000 shares. The three illustrations shown are only possible outcomes, and any of the three approaches could turn out better or worse under different market circumstances (A major disadvantage of dark pools is their lack of participation in the price discovery process. Please see Chap. 2 (Finance) for a discussion of the advantages versus disadvantages of lit versus dark markets.)

[5] "Citadel Securities, Quantlab Loom Over Trial Probing Whether Human Traders Tricked Machines," Wall Street Journal, Sept. 18, 2020

Eliminate the Middleman? – Many observers predicted that electronic markets would squeeze out dealers and other intermediaries in the financial markets. That has not turned out to be the case, and many intermediaries operate in today's markets. Investor-driven order flow provides sufficient liquidity in only a handful of the most active stocks and financial instruments. In other markets, supplemental liquidity provision is required, and dealers and market makers step in to buy or to sell when there is an imbalance in the flow of orders. Supplemental liquidity providers tend to have short holding periods and do not try to exploit large moves over long time periods. Often referred to as "scalpers," they attempt to keep inventory and position risks low while "capturing" the bid-ask spread or taking advantage of small moves that occur frequently. Today's market-making firms, however, supply liquidity with sophisticated software and analytic risk models. They employ far fewer people than these firms did in the era of floor trading when they operated as dealers such as NYSE specialists or futures market "locals." While trading costs have come down, the market depth and the quality of price discovery remain a reason trading intermediation remains desirable.

Fragmented Markets – Technology has driven a proliferation of markets and competing venues for trading. In 2020, the United States had 16 licensed equity exchanges, up from 11 in 2014, including the NYSE, Nasdaq, CBOE, and IEX, and about 50 alternative trading systems (ATSs). ATSs, which include dark pools, accounted for 40% of trading in 2019 according to Rosenblatt Securities. Off-exchange trading also goes through "wholesalers" or market makers, such as Citadel Securities and Virtu Financial, which execute retail orders for brokerage firms with the promise of providing better trading prices. While market makers may end up executing some trades on an exchange or in a dark pool, they often wind up 'internalizing' (e.g., buying for their own account when a customer sells) a large portion of the orders by taking on position risk and using their capital to complete them. The evidence suggests this competition is good for market participants, but with multiple trading venues, there are also concerns that *fragmentation* can impair price discovery and reduce liquidity and also make liquidity more difficult to access. One counterargument is that with sufficient transparency and shared market information, multiple technology-connected trading venues may effectively provide the benefits of a single, consolidated market, but the jury is still out on this one.

Computerized Trading Messaging Standards and FIX – As computerized order routing and trading began to replace phone calls and paper trading tickets in the 1980s, technologists had to work with different vendor-specific electronic communications formats and proprietary messaging standards. The NYSE, for instance, used its own message formats in its Common Message Switch (CMS) that connected traders away from the trading floor to its DOT system. The separate and incompatible interfaces for different exchanges and different brokerage firms created a need to consolidate traders' points of entry and to realize cost savings by standardizing on a single, open protocol for trade messages that was not controlled by a vendor or an exchange.

In 1992, the Financial Information eXchange (FIX) was founded as a result of a collaboration between IT teams at a "sell-side" firm (Salomon Brothers) and a "buy-side" firm (Fidelity Investments). FIX is a series of specifications for

Message:	8=FIX.4.4|9=122|35=D|34=215|49=CLIENT12|52=20100225-19:41:57.316|56=B|1=Marcel| 11=13346|21=1|40=2|44=5|54=1|59=0|60=20100225-19:39:52.020|10=072|		
Tag	Field	Value	Description
8	BeginString	FIX.4.4	Identifies beginning of new message and protocol version
9	BodyLength	122	Message length, in bytes
35	MsgType	D	NewOrderSingle
34	MsgSeqNum	215	Integer message sequence number
49	SenderCompID	CLIENT12	Identifies firm sending message
52	SendingTime	20100225-19:41:57.316	Time of message transmission
56	TargetCompID	BrokerA	Identifies receiving firm
1	Account	Marcel	Account mnemonic
11	ClOrdID	13346	Unique identifier for Order
21	HandlInst	1	Instructions for order handling: 1 = Automated execution order, private, no Broker intervention.
40	OrdType	2	Order type. 2 = Limit
44	Price	5	Price per unit of quantity (e.g. per share)
54	Side	1	Side of order. 1 = Buy
59	TimeInForce	0	Specifies how long the order remains in effect. 0 = Day
60	TransactTime	20100225-19:39:52.020	Time of execution/order creation
10	CheckSum	72	Three bytes, simple checksum

Fig. 4.8 Sample a FIX message for a limit order to buy at 5 sent by CLIENT12 to Broker A and a table describing each of the field in the tagged-field message. (From: http://www.validfix.com/fix-analyzer.html)

machine-readable messages related to securities transactions and markets and their real-time transmission among market participants. For an IT professional, managing trading applications and keeping latency low increasingly require an understanding of the FIX protocol.

A FIX message is a digital message with a list of fields with numerical tags and values separated by "|." Each tag corresponds to a different field for which a certain set of user-entered values is allowed. An example of a FIX message is presented in Fig. 4.8.

The pattern in each FIX message is Tag=Value|Tag=Value|Tag=Value|.... Depending on the purpose of each message, different sets of tags and permitted values are included. By using FIX technology in their trading applications, market participants are effectively agreeing to speak the same "language" with the markets, the exchanges that they use, and the broker-dealer counterparties that serve them.

Further Information Technology Issues – Technology and the use of the trading applications that rely on common standards such as SWIFT and FIX have made traders more productive and have reduced errors that occurred in manual trading. Nonetheless, advances and new applications of IT open complex questions for market regulators and trading organizations that are described below.

Transparency – The amount of information available from markets and the emergence of direct access to the trading process have empowered investors to manage their trading activities more closely. Pre-trade data exchanged in some markets include the identity of the firm that placed the order. However, some participants prefer anonymity to prevent their proprietary activities from being front-run or being "reverse-engineered" by other participants. Even innocuous post-trade information such as the identities of the executing broker and the clearing firms can signal what an investor or hedge fund is doing (such as building up a large position in advance of a takeover offer).

Information Disclosure – There are many types of regularly scheduled public information releases from companies, including their annual financial statements and quarterly reports. Private and insider information is more concerning since trading on privileged information can be illegal and disadvantages uninformed traders and erodes confidence in market integrity. Greater sharing and analysis of qualitative, unstructured information – such as the text of a speech or a letter to shareholders – provides heightened visibility into company activities, and this could level the playing field and reduce information asymmetries potentially harming less sophisticated investors. Hedge funds not surprisingly are at the leading edge and have developed proprietary text mining techniques to rapidly assess the positive or negative "sentiment" of speeches, news stories, or company press releases.

Complexity – As markets have innovated and competition among trading venues for order flow has grown, new complexities and challenges are emerging. In the past, the fees charged to broker-dealer firms for their trade executions were fairly uniform across stock exchanges. A new range of rebate approaches and fee models have developed to attract order flow. The use of incentives for certain order types was pioneered by the Island ECN in the late 1990s. In its maker/taker model, Island attracted limit order users by rebating $0.002 per share if their order traded and charging the market order a $0.003 per share fee. Island kept the difference. Recently, some trading venues have inverted this model to charge the limit order trader and rebate the "taker." Such incentives can lead to orders being routed *not* based on where the best price discovery and liquidity are, but on where the firm will maximize its payment for order flow. The results could be pricing distortions and publicly visible bid/offer prices in the market that are less accurate since rebates and other discounts are hidden.

System Reliability – Like other technologies, trading systems are subject to failures, breakdowns, and unanticipated responses to conditions. In 2012, a prominent market-making firm, Knight Capital, caused a major stock market disruption and suffered a $440 million trading loss. A significant error in the operation of its automated routing software for equity orders caused it, in roughly 45 minutes, to route millions of orders into the market that resulted in over 4 million trades in 154 stocks for nearly 400 million shares. For instance, the flood of orders to buy shares of Wizzard Software Corporation caused its price to move from $3.50 to $14.76. The SEC's erroneous trade rules[6] developed after the 2010 "flash crash" led to trades at least 30% away from the "reference price" being cancelled, which happened for Wizzard and five other stocks.

Knight was found to have violated SEC rules that required broker-dealers to have controls and procedures to limit the risks associated with automated trading systems and to prevent these types of errors. Mary Schapiro, the then-Securities and Exchange Commission (SEC) chairperson, recommended the voluntary guidelines – known as Automation Review Policies that have covered technological systems since the 1987

[6] See FINRA Rule 11890-Clearly Erroneous Transactions. https://www.finra.org/rules-guidance/rulebooks

crash – become mandatory: "As the SEC catches up with the realities of today's market, it seems an appropriate moment to require that every entity in an interconnected system work to ensure its capacity, resiliency, and security."

A further example occurred on Thursday, October 1, 2020, when the Tokyo Stock Exchange experienced a full day shutdown of its market when a data device malfunctioned and the switchover to the backup device failed. Testing and backup plans are crucial because of the numerous interconnections and interdependencies and because changes to components or software in one "layer" of the stack can trigger unanticipated breakdowns elsewhere.

Open Architecture and Scalability – Market systems are designed today with open architectures that make adding or upgrading components efficient. Non-proprietary approaches are more cost-effective and provide a high degree of scalability. An added benefit is not being tied into a single vendor. Today's trading platforms are built on open source software and can be deployed in many different data center and cloud environments.

4.8 Conclusion

The technology of trading has evolved rapidly, and market quality in many respects has been improved. Traders are more productive than ever, with computer algorithms handling the work of entering orders while monitoring and responding to market conditions, and trading professionals able to focus on more complex orders and formulate new strategies. A senior trader at Instinet made the following comment:

> No question, the markets are better now than ever before. Everybody agrees with that. Spreads are tighter; more volume can go through the pipes, all the exchanges compete. Indeed, there are many ways to execute a stock, and there are dark pools, and exchanges. That said, it's complicated
>
> - Anthony Fortunato, Chapter 2 in "Technology's Challenge to Regulators: *40 Years of Experience with the National Market System (NMS): Who Are the Winners and What Have We Learned?*" Schwartz, R., J. Byrne, and E. Stempel, eds., Springer, forthcoming, 2021

In spite of the complexity, the following facets of IT are of fundamental importance in trading environments:

System Reliability – Shutdowns of financial trading make front page news and often lead to political interventions. Surging trading volumes in the late 1960s led to a paperwork crisis in US stock markets as a backlog of unsettled trades built up. To address the problem, US equity markets were closed on Wednesdays from mid-1968 to early 1969. In response, both the US Senate and House held hearings on the matter and, in consultation with the SEC, drafted legislation to deal with the paperwork crisis. In 1972 and 1973, the National Securities Clearing Corp. and Depository Trust Company were established to provide computerized, "book-entry" transfer of ownership and to reduce the movement of paper securities certificates. But the reliability of the trading systems themselves is of tremendous importance.

Open Architecture – Non-proprietary technology and vendor-neutral standards are preferred in financial markets. Open architectures enable innovations by market participants and foster competition among technology vendors to improve components in each layer of the "stack."

Scalability – Trading volumes fluctuate widely in equity markets. Peak trading volumes can be 100 times larger than average volumes, and a news announcement about a company or an update from the Federal Reserve chair can lead to a spike in trading. Market capacity needs to be able to scale up rapidly in order to handle the occasional bursts of heavy market activity without disruption or significantly increasing latency. In addition, an exchange must be able to handle an order flow that, over time, continues an upward trending.

In this chapter, we have focused on the critical skills and the necessary understanding of technology applications in financial markets. The foundational components of IT systems were presented along with issues of market regulation and risk management. We identified how IT streamlines and reduces costs for existing institutions but also provides a platform for innovators and start-ups seeking to compete and disrupt powerful incumbent organizations. This background is intended to help you to become a confident technologist who can analyze data and make decisions regarding how to react to today's financial market trends.

Financial markets have long histories, but the economic forces underlying markets are little changed from the 1700s when the precursors of the London Stock Exchange and the New York Stock Exchange were established at Jonathan's Coffee House (1761) and under a buttonwood tree (1792). Although IT is well-known as a transformational force in markets, research and teaching in the academic fields of IS and Finance are just beginning to adequately describe the optimal strategies for deploying IT in financial markets to reduce trading costs and improve liquidity. Consequently, this chapter has identified the major transformational impacts that IT has had and presented a foundation for understanding the strategic technologies essential for managing financial firms and competing successfully in today's capital markets.

Experiencing Market Dynamics with TraderEx: A Trading Decision-Making Simulation

5

We have presented the case in this book that *trading* education is important for success in the securities and investments industry. Are apprenticeships and time on an institutional trading desk the only way to learn how to trade? Do you need to work with real orders and have real money at risk to gain experience interacting with the dynamic process of price formation? The answers are no and no. Trading simulations that are well-designed can create experiences with price discovery and impose the challenges of illiquidity in ways that replicate the learning accomplished (and pressures felt) on a real trading desk. With TraderEx, you will appreciate the complexity of trading and understand it as a distinct profession within the financial industry, even if it is not always thought of as such in business school curriculum.[1]

Our years of experience teaching with the TraderEx trading simulation system have shown that it is an excellent way to "bring to life" many of the concepts presented in this book. TraderEx creates a market order flow and a realistic environment in which you can experience how price discovery takes place and liquidity fluctuates. You will observe and understand that you should trade differently under different market structures. TraderEx can be played solo in a solitaire session or in the advanced version, trading can occur among multiple players in a networked session. It accommodates the three main types of market structures that we have discussed in the previous chapters: order-driven, quote-driven, and call auction.

In this section, we focus on four critical realities that can be brought to life via TraderEx. The TraderEx simulation is intended to enable you to:

- Understand that market prices commonly do not equal equilibrium values.
- Find out how your own trading decisions can impact market prices.

[1] The software for TraderEx current version was developed by Andrew Novocin, Ph.D., in JavaScript and Firebase, a cloud-hosted database. The statistical model used in TraderEx was developed by Schwartz and Weber and first implemented in SimScript II.5 in 1991.

D. Ozenbas et al., *Liquidity, Markets and Trading in Action*, Classroom Companion: Business, https://doi.org/10.1007/978-3-030-74817-3_5

- Experience the varied environments of different market structures (i.e., market structure matters).
- Assess the costs of illiquidity – In a highly liquid market, trading is cheap and easy, but markets are commonly less than perfectly liquid.

Our focus in this chapter will be the order-driven market structure. In this structure, the orders of some participants establish the prices at which other participants can trade. Any participant can "supply" liquidity by entering limit orders or can "consume" liquidity with market orders. This differs from a "quote driven" market where dealer quotes establish the prices at which other participants can trade. In a pure dealer market, the dealers are the only source of liquidity, and other participants trade at the dealer quotes (by placing market orders) only.

Order-driven markets have two forms: "continuous" and "periodic." Continuous means that a trade can be made at any point in continuous time when a buy order matches or crosses a sell order in price. For example, if you are willing to buy 100 shares at a $20 limit price while I am willing to sell 100 shares now at $20 and our orders meet when the market is open, a trade will occur.

Periodic trading is referred to as "call auction trading." In the call auction environment, orders are not executed even if they meet or cross in price until the market is "called." The call and continuous market structures offer different advantages, and in today's electronic exchanges, they are generally combined in a hybrid market environment. To keep things simple, we will focus on continuous market trading only in this chapter.

5.1 Conceptual Features of the TraderEx Trading Simulation

Trading simulations enable you to gain experience making trading decisions without risking actual money. TraderEx provides a market structure, which is the set of rules for matching buy and sell orders to create trades, and the software generates a stream of orders. To be realistic and engaging, a trading simulation must have four properties:

1. The computer-generated order flow must capture the pricing dynamics of a real-world marketplace.
2. The simulated market must give you some basis for anticipating future price movements.
3. The software must enable you to replay a simulation run so that you can see the effect of a change of your strategy, or of the market structure, or of the parameter settings (e.g., volatility, order arrival rate, etc.)
4. The simulation must provide you with meaningful performance benchmarks to compare with others and to get feedback on how you are improving with experience.

TraderEx's computer-generated order flow is based on draws from various statistical distributions. The most important determinant of the market's dynamics is the equilibrium price, which we call P* ("P-star"). P_t* is the valuation at time t of the stock based on full information and no economic frictions. Of course, new information arrives over time that affects the P* value, but these shocks are unpredictable and the changes that raise and lower the equilibrium value are balanced, making the evolution of P* a driftless random walk process. In a hypothetical world with costless trading and complete, instantaneous information dissemination, price adjustments are instantaneous, one-shot events. The market price would always be P*. In real-world markets, informationally motivated orders arrive at the market sequentially, and price adjustments are noisy and non-instantaneous.

Along with the simulation's random information events and their changes in the stock's underlying value (P*), there are economic forces driving the three classes of traders in the simulation:

Informed traders: they are motivated to trade by the arrival of news that causes P* to be greater than market prices (informed buying) or to be less than market prices (informed selling).

Liquidity traders: they are motivated by their own cash flow needs and individual, uninformed reassessments of share value.

Technical traders: they are motivated by their beliefs that they have observed exploitable patterns in the stock's price movements.

The arrival rates for orders and events can be modeled as statistical processes. The arrivals of information-driven and liquidity-driven orders are modeled with the use of a stochastic process known as the Poisson arrival process. What moves the market into alignment with P* is the one-sided trading of informed participants. When the P* valuation is greater (or less) than the stock's market price, informed orders are motivated to buy (sell) and will continue to trade in a single direction until market quotes straddle P*. For example, if P* is $22.50 and the market bid-ask is $22.40–$22.60, there is no informed trading opportunity, but if P* jumps above the $22.60 ask, informed buy orders will kick in until the market price rises to the level of P*. If P* drops below the $22.40 bid, informed sell orders will kick in. In TraderEx, price changes reflecting new information take place sequentially, and consequently, with liquidity and technical traders also on the scene, realized transaction prices are blurred and noisy signals of P*.

The magnitude of information change, when it occurs, is reflected in the size of the jump in the fundamental value, P*. Each change in P* is an investment return to holders of the stock. P* jumping up (a positive return) is good news that means that the stock has a greater value, while P* dropping down (a negative return) is bad news for holders of the stock. In our TraderEx simulation, the P* returns are lognormally distributed with a mean of zero as the default setting.

Over any simulation run, P* may drift up or it may drift down, but with a mean return of zero, there is no systematic tendency for it to move in one direction or the other over any simulation run. We can change the impact of the information events, and thus the underlying level of market volatility, by changing the variance parameter of the lognormal return distribution. Because the P* returns are obtained by random draw, successive changes in P* are not serially correlated. That is, P* moves randomly through time, and thus, our equilibrium price follows a random walk.

When P* is above the offer (or below the bid), the arrival rate of market orders to buy (or to sell) is increased from 50% to 67% of the total order flow. When P* is below the bid, there will be, on average, twice as many sell orders as buy orders, and when P* is above the offer, there will be, on average, twice the number of buy orders as sell orders. When P* is between the bid and the offer, no informed orders are generated, and market orders to buy and to sell are entered by liquidity traders with equal probability.

The liquidity orders in TraderEx are equally likely to be buy orders or sell orders, and the assignment for each newly generated liquidity order is done randomly and independently. Whatever motivates them, the important thing for us is that these orders are uncorrelated with each other and with the information orders. Recognizing this, the "liquidity motive" includes all reasons that are unique to an individual and represent each trader's own, individual reassessment of share value.

TraderEx incorporates a type of technical trader, a momentum player. Momentum trading is an essential component of TraderEx. Without some noise from uninformed traders, it would be too easy for you to detect P* shifts from the evolution of trade prices. This is because any jump in P* that puts it above the offer (or below the bid) triggers a preponderance of machine-generated market orders to buy (or market orders to sell), and these market orders cause prices to run up (or to run down) toward the new value of P*, but then stop once prices are again in equilibrium. This pattern must be obscured in some way, or you could profit too easily by buying or selling whenever price appears to be trending up or down. We do not want you to be a monopolist with respect to this strategy, and momentum trading is the answer because it will compete with you if you try to jump on a trend by buying when the quotes rise or by selling when they fall.

Further, with momentum traders on board, trends can be misleading. The momentum-driven orders raise uncertainty for you by reinforcing false, unsustainable price moves that are not driven by P*. Prices in TraderEx can trend up due to several liquidity-motivated buy orders arriving by chance. And the overshooting relative to P* caused by momentum orders is necessary for limit orders to be submitted. This is because overshooting enables a larger set of limit orders to execute, not just those at the best bid and offer, and for the limit order placer to profit from price then reverting back toward its previous level. A relatively wide bid-ask spread also provides this kind of compensation. In other words, the TraderEx simulation mimics the ecology of a real-world stock market where different traders trade based on their varied motives and expectations.

5.2 Using the TraderEx Trading Simulation

The most straightforward way to use the TraderEx system if you are on your own is to use the "Order Book" version and by clicking the "Solitaire Session" option. This limited functionality version is available at https://demo.etraderex.com/ (Exhibit 5.1a).

When you click the start arrow "→]" displayed in Exhibit 5.1b, the system will initiate the simulation and automatically populate the order book with limit orders like the one described in detail in the Finance chapter. Once you press the red "Start" button, the system clock will start, and you will see dynamic updates to the order book as orders from the computer program (and in the networked version when live participants) arrive. An image of this limit order book is presented in Exhibit 5.2.

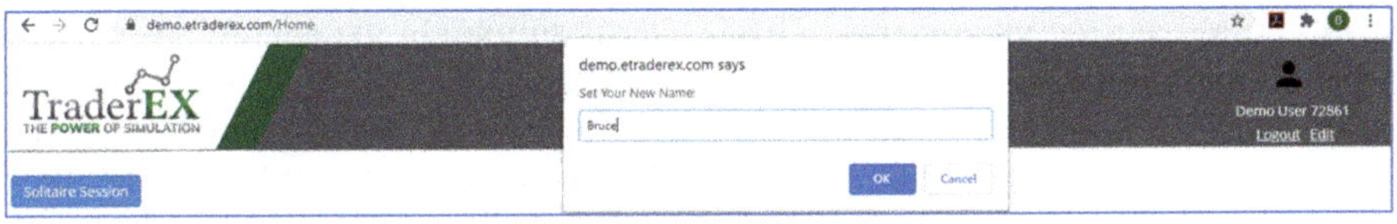

Exhibit 5.1a TraderEx landing page after selecting "Sign In Anonymously"

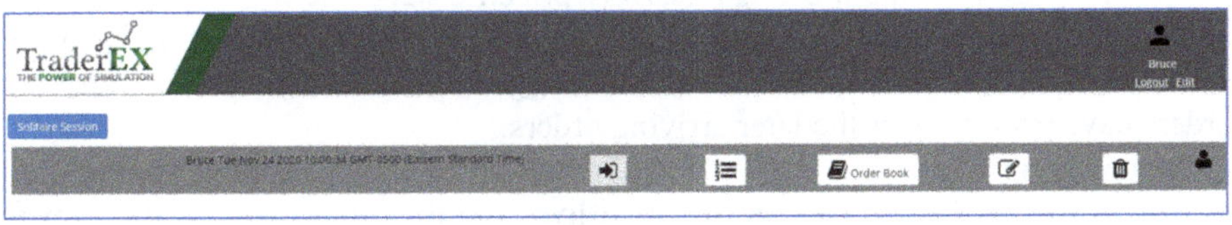

Exhibit 5.1b After using "Edit" to enter your name, click on "Solitaire Session" to create a single-use order book simulation

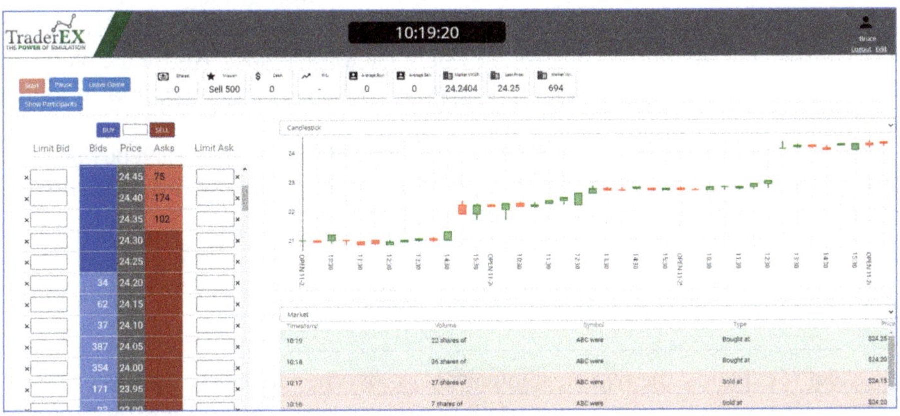

Exhibit 5.2 Limit order book from TraderEx simulation

Exhibit 5.2 displays a set of orders that drive a continuous, order-driven market. The left-hand side shows orders that have been posted on "the book." The book is the market. It has three columns: the middle column displays a price ladder (from the highest down to the lowest); the column to the left shows, at each price, the number of shares sought for purchase (a share in TraderEx is a "round lot" that corresponds to 100 shares in an actual stock market); and the column to the right of the price ladder shows, at each price, the number of shares offered for sale. The chart shows three prior days of simulated price action with a Candlestick display that shows green or red every 30 min depending on whether the price rose or fell in that time window.

Look at the blue, gray, and red columns on the left of Exhibit 5.2. What strikes you? Notice that the selling prices are all higher than the buying prices. Why, you might ask, has no seller stated a willingness to offer shares at a price lower than the most aggressive buyer is willing to pay, or that no buyer is willing to purchase shares at a price higher than the most aggressive seller has offered to part with shares at? What accounts for this? The answer is simple. In the continuous market, a trade occurs if the prices stated on a buy order and on a sell order meet or cross. As the trade is being made, these orders are "executed," and executed orders no longer appear on the book. The book, therefore, contains only sell limit orders that are posted above the limit buys and buy limit orders that are posted below the limit sells. In TraderEx, when there are multiple limit orders making up the displayed quantity at a price, the priority rules for which orders trade kick in. The first priority rule is price priority: the most aggressively priced orders (the highest priced buys and the lowest priced sells) execute first. The second priority rule is time priority: when multiple orders are at the same most aggressive price, the earliest arriving orders have priority over the later arriving orders.

Below the price chart in Exhibit 5.2, TraderEx provides a scrolling blotter of all trading in the market. Trades are reported live, and then they scroll down as new trades occur. The blotter entries are either green or red, with green indicating trades that were triggered by arriving buy orders that executed against limit orders to sell that were resting in the book. Red rows show trades that were triggered by sell orders arriving and executing against buy orders that were resting on the book. By clicking on the rectangle above the blotter, you can toggle between Market and User, which will filter the blotter to show only the user's trades. Above the blotter is a price chart with 3 days of price information. The chart allows the user to toggle between a Candlestick display and a Line display.

Once you comfortably understand how the book displays the posted buy and sell orders, let us enter this market and trade. But first, doing so requires knowing the order types available to you and how to submit them.

5.3 Orders Types

As Chap. 2 explains, the two most important order types are market orders and limit orders. We can think of limit orders as "price contingent orders." They trade (or not) contingent on the market price reaching the limit price and a counterparty order arriving. A multiplicity of other order types exists – stop orders, market-on-close orders, hidden orders, etc. – but they are not essential to the operations of an order-driven market. Market and limit orders are essential. Let us focus on them.

We have discussed Exhibit 5.2 and how buy and sell orders are posted on either side of the price ladder. Are these limit orders or market orders? Consider the buy orders at 30.65 and 30.55, which summed together are for 75 TraderEx shares. What kind of orders are these? Answer: limit orders. Why are they called "limit orders"? First, these are priced orders – the prices being \$30.65 and \$30.55. What is each price saying? According to the first trader's instruction, those 6 shares should be bought at any price of \$30.65 or lower. In other words, \$30.65 is the maximum the buyer is willing to pay. As a maximum, it is setting a limit: "I am willing to pay up to \$30.65 but not a nickel more."

What about on the sell side? The interpretation of a posted sell order is the same as that of a posted buy order, but with one exception: the price limit on a sell order is a minimum, not a maximum. For instance, the sell orders placed at a price of \$30.85 account for a total of 59 shares that are for sale only if they can be sold at a price of \$30.85 or higher (but not for one nickel less!).

Conclusion: limit orders are called because they are priced, and the prices are limits: a maximum limit for buy orders and a minimum limit for sell orders. To solidify your grasp of these maximum and minimum limits, refer back to Exhibit 5.2 and calculate the total number of shares that, given the book, can be bought up to a price of \$30.90 or sold down to a price of \$30.50 (A: 172 and 138).

Let us introduce some additional terminologies.

- Limit order book: We have been referring to the columns on the left-hand side of Exhibit 5.2 as the "book." Because the book contains limit orders, it is commonly referred to as the "limit order book."
- Quotes: The prices of the most aggressively priced orders (highest priced buy order and lowest priced sell order) on the book are commonly referred to as "quotes."
- Offer price: This term is sometimes used instead of "ask" price.
- Best bid and offer: This is sometimes referred to as the BBO or the "inside market," or as the "inside quotes."
- Bid-ask spread: The lowest ask quote minus the highest bid quote is the spread.

On to market orders. You have an alternative to entering limit orders in the TraderEx marketplace. You can also submit market orders. This is an unpriced order that reflects a simple statement: "I want to buy or to sell X number of shares at the market price." When submitting a market order, you would certainly want to know what the best prices on the book are, for these prices define "the market."

So look again at Exhibit 5.2 and identify the best price that a market order to buy or to sell would transact at. Answer: the lowest ask price (for a buy order) and the highest bid price (for a sell order). However, we point out two provisos. First, if you enter a market order for a larger number of shares than the number posted at the best bid or ask, it will execute only partially at this best price, and the remainder will "walk the book" to less aggressive prices (up the book for a larger buy order and down the book for a larger sell order). The second proviso is that while you are in the process of submitting your order, some other orders may shoot in ahead of you, transact against the book, and result in your order executing at a price inferior to what you had expected. If that happens to you while playing TraderEx, you will better understand why equity market traders put great value on the speed with which they can get information and act on it.

5.4 Running a TraderEx Simulation

Let us go ahead and complete an instruction: buy 500 shares over the course of one trading day (9:30–16:00). Looking at Exhibit 5.3, we see that buying the full order immediately by market order would "crash through" the 20.90 and 20.95 bids and drive the price up down to $21.00. To avoid that costly market impact, we enter a market order to buy 12 from the limit orders to sell and place a limit order to buy at $20.85.

In TraderEx, you begin the day with a zero share position and zero cash, and no commissions are charged. This keeps the focus on your trading and the prices you realize. Our market order to buy 12 shares executed at $20.95 at 9:39. We have an obligation to pay and therefore have a cash position of -$251.40. Notice that TraderEx computes a P/L (profit and loss) using a "mark-to-market" formula. Mark-to-market of a short position is done by multiplying the share position by the current best ask and subtracting that from what was generated when we sold the shares. We, however, are long 12 shares and will mark to market at the highest bid to calculate the revenue from selling the 12 shares. That is 12×20.85 = $250.2 and therefore, our P/L is –$0.60 $60.00 if we factor in that these are round lots of 100.

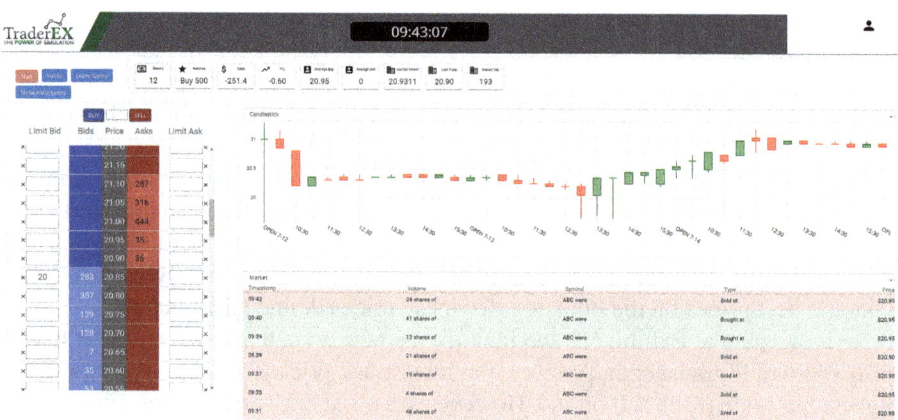

Exhibit 5.3 Limit order book from TraderEx simulation - The user's instruction is to Buy 500 by the end of the trading day

Over the rest of the trading day, how do we know how we are doing as we execute our sell orders? A number of transaction cost analysis methods exist, but we will focus on one – VWAP benchmarking. VWAP stands for volume weighted average price and is calculated by dividing the total value of trades during the day by the number of shares traded. For example, if 100 shares trade at $20.00 and 300 shares trade at $19.80, the VWAP is $19.85.[2] To complete an instruction to buy a large quantity over the course of a day and pay an average price per share that is less than VWAP is an accomplishment. Similarly completing a large number of sell orders and finishing with an average price per share sold above the VWAP is a success.

Exhibit 5.4 shows the situation at 1:58 pm. We have bought 380 shares and have resting limit orders for 45 of the remaining 120. The average buying price we have paid so far is $21.4293, and the VWAP is $21.2676. In what has been a rising market, we have paid about 16 cents more than VWAP. So far, not so good, but two more hours of trading remains.

The end-of-day display in Exhibit 5.5 shows that 6,093 shares traded, and the last trade was at $21.20. Our trading (500) made up about 8% of the day's volume. Our buying prices averaged $21.4078 per share compared to the market VWAP of $21.3077. We finished our instruction to buy 500 and were not able to improve on the VWAP price. In a difficult, rising market, we bought for 10 cent more than VWAP. We'll do better next time. Those 10 cents will reduce whatever returns result from holding these 500 shares. If we had been able to buy 10 cents *below* VWAP, we would add $0.10 ÷ $21.3077 = +0.47% to the performance of the investor from this stock holding.

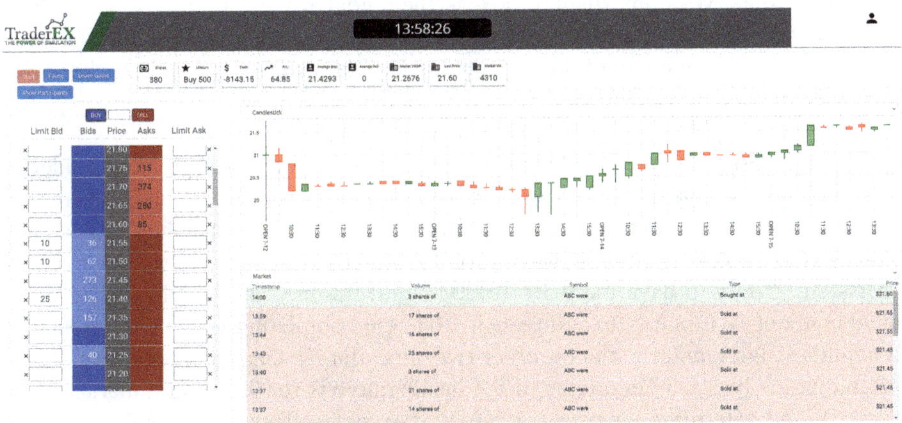

Exhibit 5.4 About two hours remain in the TraderEx simulation

[2] The VWAP calculation is Value Traded ($) ÷ Volume Traded (shares) = (100×$20.00 + 300×$19.80) ÷ (100+300) = $19.85.

Exhibit 5.5 End of the simulated day of trading

Notice also that the P/L is negative. To see why this is, consider that our buying 500 at an average price of $20.4078 cost us $10,703.90. The last price in the market was 21.20, so selling 500 at that price would generate 10,600, and therefore, we have a P/L of 10,703.90–10,600 = –$103.90

To recap, we played the TraderEx simulation as a buy-side trader with a mandate to buy or to sell a certain number of shares during the trading day.[3] Typically, traders who work for an investment management firm would have an instruction or ("mission") to buy or to sell a specific number of shares to help the fund under their management accumulate or reduce a position for their investors. These participants are the "buy-side" traders. In this case, as shown in Exhibit 5.5, the player used the number in the "Mission" display box as their goal for the trading day. For this example, the Mission box indicated "Buy 500," and the trader bought 500 shares of the security before the end of the trading day and, unfortunately paid a higher price than VWAP.

Exercise 1 Go to the website (https://demo.etraderex.com/) and create a TraderEx Solitaire Session. Then launch the simulation with the right arrow icon. There will be a slight delay initializing the simulated market before the Start button is active. You will be given a mission to buy or to sell a certain quantity shown under "Mission." You will have the 9:30–16:00 (4 pm) trading day, which will be simulated in about 10 minutes, to complete it. To begin completing your instruction after the market starts, enter a market order two times larger than the number of shares offered at the best market quotes (if the inside quote is for 90, enter a market order for 180) and determine the prices at which it executes. This will probably not be a good trade for you because of market impact, which has been referred to as the "price concession an investor may be forced to make for trading in quantities greater than those associated with the posted bid or ask price." In the TraderEx marketplace,

[3] More detailed definitions of the buy- and sell-side participants can be found in Chap. 2.

you will have market impact if you bang into the book with sufficiently large market orders. The orders that you executed are displayed by clicking on "User" at the bottom of the price chart on the screen. Continue trading to reach your target position. The market will close at 4 pm. How did you do? Did you acquire the target position? How does your average price for selling or buying compare to VWAP?

Exercise 2 Repeat Exercise 1 but without placing the large initial market order. Did you improve your outcome when you did not start the day with a large market order?

Exercise 3 A player can also participate in the game by placing limit buy (or "bid") orders on the left-side column and limit sell (or "ask") orders in the right-side column. In Exhibit 5.6, you have placed 80 shares to buy at a limit price of $21.45 and 90 shares to sell at $20.60. This type of order placement strategy could be effective for those playing the game as a proprietary trader or "market maker" whose goal is to capture the $0.15 spread between their bid and ask while not letting their positions get too large and risky. Most "prop traders" want to finish the day with a "flat book" or zero position in the stock to avoid overnight risk. If successful, you might be able to make round-trip profits of $0.15 per share. What could go wrong? To find out, start a new TraderEx session and run it. Ignore the "Mission" that is provided and seek to earn trading profits by two-sided trading to capture the spread. Bring your position back to zero by the market close at 16:00. How did you do in terms of P&L and the number of shares that you traded? What else may have affected your trading? The size of the spread, risk/position size, time remaining in the trading day? Anything else?

Exhibit 5.6 A market making strategy to earn trading profit from posting two-way limit orders to both buy and sell

Exercise 4 An alternative strategy is to study short-term market momentum and use the "Buy" and "Sell" buttons at the top of Exhibit 5.6 to place market orders when you see the market trending up or down. For instance, if the bid rises to a new, higher level that suggests buying pressure is building, then enter a market order to buy. Later you hope to sell your newly bought shares at a higher price. Although market orders execute swiftly, the downside is that you pay the bid-ask spread on any round-trip trade (i.e., you buy at the higher ask price and then sell at the lower bid price). Market orders are best used by players who need to act quickly on new information, or who are looking to close out their positions so that, at the end of the day, they are neither long nor short the security. If you are playing the game as a trend follower or speculator, then it might be worth paying the bid-ask spread by placing a market order if it helps you catch a short-term trend in the market. Create a new TraderEx session and run it. Ignore the "Mission" that is provided and seek out trading profits by trading with market orders when an uptrend or downtrend emerges. Bring your position back to zero by the market's 16:00 close.

5.5 Diving Deeper

After the TraderEx simulation is completed for the trading day, you can click the results icon ("1., 2., 3.") Orde to see how you performed relative to your goals. For example, a buy-side trader's shares should reflect their mission, and ideally, the average price will be close to or better than the market VWAP (Exhibit 5.7).

At the end of a trading session, a buy-side trader should have a position equal to the number of shares displayed in the Mission box (and, of course, with the correct sign). That is, the buy-side trader should finish with +500 shares if the Mission box indicates "Buy 500" and, conversely, with –500 shares if the Mission box displays "Sell 500." These buy-side traders can then be evaluated according to their Buy VWAP (average buy price) vis-à-vis the market's overall average price (Market VWAP). When their mission is to "buy," it is a good result when their "average buy" price is lower than the market's VWAP. In contrast, if their mission is to "sell," then their "average sell" price should be higher than the Market VWAP. In contrast, a market maker's net position should be zero at the end of the day while ideally earning a positive profit (as shown by the "Shares" and "P/L" columns). A trend-following proprietary trader might also finish with a zero position, and show a positive P/L (profit/loss) if they made

Export Summary Data | Export Your Trades | Export All Player Trades | Display Chart

#	User	Shares	Mission	P/L	BuyVWAP	SellVWAP	MarketVWAP
1	BRUCE	500	Buy 500	-228.9000	21.4078	-	21.3077

Exhibit 5.7 Post-simulation results – the seller completed the instruction

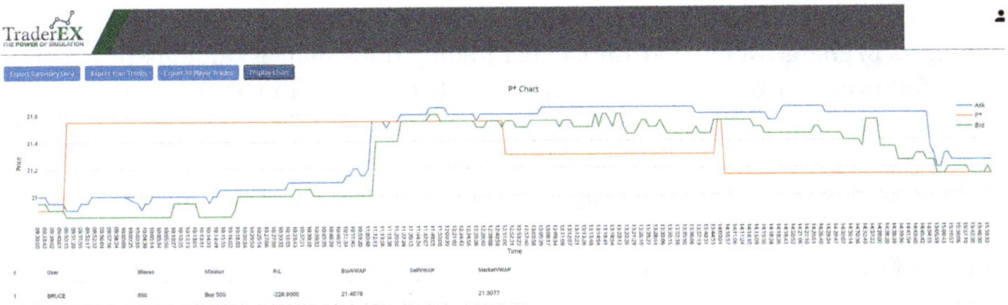

Exhibit 5.8 Post-simulation price chart – the bid and ask quotes and P* over the trading day

trades early in any up- or downtrends during the day and closed out before the trend is reversed.

The chart that a TraderEx user can display (Exhibit 5.8) shows the evolution of the market quotes and P* over the course of the trading day. Notice that it takes some time for the informed trading activity to move the price into alignment with P*. For a trader with a buy instruction, the best prices were available early in the day. A trend trader could have profited by buying at 20.20 or so before the price rose to 21. Of course not every price pattern will be advantageous to a trend-following buyer.

After reviewing these results and the chart, it is usually good to re-run the simulation and see if you can improve with a new and different P* path that will almost certainly impact the results you realize.

To review, we completed a large buy or sell order as a buy-side trader in Exercises 1 and 2. In Exercise 3, you traded like a market maker who wants (1) to capture the bid-ask spread by placing limit buy orders below the limit sell orders and, ideally, (2) to transact frequently throughout the day while ending the day with a net zero position (i.e., be neither long nor short the security). Such proprietary traders and speculators usually want to end the day with a zero position, but they are willing to place limit orders on one side of the market (either long or short) for a longer period during the day if they want to bear some uncertain and accept potentially greater position risk. In Exercise 4, you explored the strategy of trying to capture short-term price trends by entering market orders at times when you think prices might be about to make a move upward or downward. In contrast to short-term price speculators, buy-side traders will typically be more patient than proprietary traders and will place limit orders either to build up or to wind down a position based on the system-provided "Mission" objective.

5.6 Conclusion

The TraderEx simulation is an effective learning tool to understand trading and price discovery firsthand while receiving performance feedback on the effectiveness of your decisions. As we have described, effective buy-side trading (e.g., acquiring a position at prices less than VWAP) enhances the investment returns of the money managers in charge of the portfolio. Other trading roles such as liquidity provider or trend follower can be tried out in TraderEx. It provides a market experience that imposes illiquidity costs and exposes you to risk. These experiences replicate some of the learning and pressures felt on a real trading desk.

Simulations are an excellent way to "bring to life" many of the financial markets concepts presented in this book. While trading a single fictitious stock over the course of one day cannot capture every aspect of the professional life of a trader, it does offer a helpful introduction, and it provides a good taste of what it is like to be operating at an institutional trading desk.

Index

D. Ozenbas et al., *Liquidity, Markets and Trading in Action*, Classroom Companion: Business, https://doi.org/10.1007/978-3-030-74817-3

CPSIA information can be obtained
at www.ICGtesting.com
Printed in the USA
LVHW080445140921
697767LV00002B/72

9 783030 748166